SOME EVEN
VOLUNTEERED

Illustration by Pamela Lenck Bradford. Copyright © 1993 by Pamela Lenck Bradford

SOME EVEN VOLUNTEERED

THE FIRST WOLFHOUNDS PACIFY VIETNAM

ALFRED S. BRADFORD

 PRAEGER

Westport, Connecticut
London

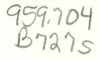

ISBN: 0-275-94785-8

Praeger Publishers, 88 Post Road West, Westport, CT 06881
An imprint of Greenwood Publishing Group, Inc.

Printed in the United States of America

98/9

To
First Lieutenant James Artman, 1/27th Infantry
Killed in Action, 28 December 1968
and
Specialist Fourth Class Miles Touchberry, 1/27th Infantry
Killed in Action, 9 April 1969

CONTENTS

MAPS

INTRODUCTION

On 24 October 1968, American troops were airlifted into an NVA rest area south of Dau Tieng. The American troops had been ordered to interdict the NVA supply line which stretched from the Ho Chi Minh trail in Cambodia through Dau Tieng to Saigon. The troops were expected to complete their mission in three days, but they uncovered such an extensive network of headquarters, hospitals, supply, troop concentrations, and local support that the mission was extended to a week, then to a month, and finally to eight months.

The NVA had promised the local inhabitants that American troops would never come to their village. When the Americans came anyway, the NVA vowed to drive them out. They calculated that a battalion could not be resupplied by air for more than a few days and could not be resupplied by road at all, but they were unable to close the road and they determined to drive the Americans away by an assault on their fire support base.

The American troops were the First Battalion of the Twenty-Seventh Infantry (First Wolfhounds). The Twenty-Seventh Infantry had been created during World War I. Its first mission, during which it won its nickname, "the Wolfhounds," had been in Russia . . . to stop the Russian Revolution ("First to Fight Communism"). The Wolfhounds had served in the Pacific in World War II and then in the Korean Conflict. In Korea the Wolfhounds gained their reputation as a first-rate fighting unit. The reputation is deserved. The First Wolfhounds (part of the 25th Infantry Division) had the highest body count of any rifle battalion in Vietnam.

In the eight-month operation (24 October 1968–9 June 1969) at Dau Tieng, the Wolfhounds made almost daily contact with the NVA. Their convoy had to fight its way up and down the road every day for five weeks, their fire support base was assaulted three times, their Brigade base was assaulted twice, they established four independent forts, they ran missions throughout the Third Brigade Area of Operations (the Michelin rubber plantation, the "Iron Triangle," the "Angel's Wing," the "Parrot's Beak"), they accepted the surrender of dozens of VC and NVA, and they killed close to a thousand NVA. By the end of the eight-month mission the Wolfhounds had destroyed, in effect, an NVA unit of their own size.

For most of that period I was the Battalion S-5 (Civic Action Officer). I went into the field, I participated in the fighting, and I attempted to win over the civilian population.

PART I

Trained to Kill

(September 1967–August 1968)

Youth-in-Asia

A little bird in the White House said,
"Ho Chi Minh, you're Russki red—
  I'm afraid you'll have to go."
  But Uncle Ho said no.
PUNCHLINE: Fifty-eight thousand Americans dead.

Chapter 1

KILLER COLLEGE

All Infantry officers who earn their bars in college (ROTC) or in the field (direct commission) must proceed to Ft. Benning, Georgia, Home of the Infantry, Queen of Battles and pass through the Infantry Officers Basic Course—IOBC. IOBC once was known by the honest acronym CPLC— Combat Platoon Leaders Course—but mothers complained that they didn't want their boys to be trained for combat and the title was changed.

While I was going through IOBC, a reporter from England visited Ft. Benning. She had asked the Brass if she could do an in-depth article on the Infantry School and the Brass had jumped at the chance to win a few British hearts and minds. They assigned a Public Information Officer to squire her all around. She was introduced to handsome young heroes, she visited the training sites, she interviewed G.I.'s and generals, she rode in a helicopter and an APC (armored personnel carrier), and she saw the film set of *The Green Berets* (then in production at Benning). When she had gathered her information, she said cheerio, chin-chin and flew back to England, where her article appeared:

HOW AMERICA TRAINS ITS KILLERS!

The Public Information Officer received a set of orders stamped "Republic of Vietnam."

We called Ft. Benning KILLER COLLEGE.

"I killed two hundred NVA with one hand," an instructor said.

"How, sir?" we asked.

He lifted an imaginary phone to his ear and said,

"Red Leg [i.e., Artillery], this is Doughboy. Fire mission. Over."

We loved war stories. Even before we (ROTC officers) had gone to war, we imagined ourselves back, telling our own stories to an awe-stricken audience. After all, Vietnam was our generation's great adventure and we had volunteered for it; we wanted to go to war. Training, however, was not war—it seemed to be a game of Cowboys and Indians, and we couldn't take it seriously. The instructors tried to get through to us with one bare statement:

"Listen up, gentlemen, or you will die in Vietnam."

The Direct Commissions (all Vietnam veterans) thought that ROTC officers were babes in the woods. We thought that they were perverse.

"I guess I'm a real gung-ho combat veteran," one of them said, after we had had a class on the M-16. "As soon as I saw that little black rifle I got a hard-on."

"That's funny—so did I," another vet said.

So had they all.

("Are we going to be like that after our tour?")

On Saturday night, when we ROTC-types were drinking Cokes and talking about our college days, the Direct Commissions were getting into fights at the American Legion Club.

"I don't like the way you're dancing with that woman!"

"Oh, yeah?"

"Yeah!"

POW!

And Dancing Boy had his upper lip split all the way to his nose.

Benning, to us, was just another college . . . with P-T and firearms. We lived in comfortable rooms, two to a room, in a building much like a dormitory; the dorm had a rec room with machines for Coke and candy. The candy machine regularly swallowed our money and refused to deliver any candy, and regularly, the first week, polite little notes appeared —this machine owes me 5¢.

In the second week, however, we had gone without sleep, we had had our first lessons in being aggressive, and we had been issued rifles. The candy machine laughed once too often.

"You son of a bitch!"

(Vertical butt stroke to the face of the machine.)

"Gentlemen," our company commander told us, "if you continue to wreck the pogey machine, it will be removed."

"If that machine cheats me," came a voice from the ranks, "it won't have to go to Vietnam to die."

Our life was simple. At reveille—the crack of dawn—we'd tumble out of the rack, eat breakfast, truck to a problem site for a lecture—"Listen up, gentlemen, today we are going to discuss artillery. It could save your life in Vietnam"—and then we'd go up the hill, down the hill, around the hill. Lunch. Zippo warfare. If it's alive, kill it. If it's not, burn it. If it won't burn, blow it up. Home, dinner, sleep.

We loved it.

Halfway through IOBC we were introduced to the Rangers. We all wanted to be Rangers: Climb mountains, eat rattlesnakes, live hard, and wear a red beanie.

"This is a rabbit snare, gentlemen," our instructor, Ranger Lieutenant Dracula, said. "You catch a rabbit, you cut its throat and drain the blood, and, gentlemen, you do not throw the blood away . . ."

He paused for effect.

". . . you drink it!"

"What about tularemia?" a learned IOBCer asked.

"Huh?"

"Ultimate tularemia."

Ranger Lieutenant Dracula did not like us; he thought we were wimps and he ran us all day, until our tongues were slapping against our ankles, and he ran us all night.

We have grown unaccustomed to the dark, what with the invention of electricity and all; college graduates—that is, Rot-C officers—are supposed to be especially inept. Someone would walk too fast, someone would walk too slow, someone would trip and fall, someone would talk, and the man on point, as I found out, soon learned that in the darkness flat land looks broken and broken land looks flat.

"College Boys!" Lt. Dracula sneered. (He had gone through OCS.) "You sound like a troop of Girl Scouts. It's sure a good thing you don't have live ammunition."

"You're right there," said a voice in the ranks.

When I hesitated before a suspicious tangle of wait-a-minute vines and deep shadow, Lt. Dracula bustled up.

"What's the delay?"

"Looks like a drop-off."

"Hell, you can't tell that at night. You're just afraid of the thorns. You've gotta push on through."

He pushed on through to show me how . . . and fell into an eight-foot-deep ditch. We laughed. He dragged himself out, assumed the lead —to set us straight—and got us lost.

"Ranger!" the voice in the ranks called out.

But we found our way at last and soon thereafter were sitting in the bleachers at a night attack problem site, where we heard how to attack a prepared position in the dark.

"Listen up, gentlemen, if you don't want to die in Vietnam."

As we left the bleachers to draw up our plans for the night attack practical exercise, rain came down in torrents.

"It's raining," an acute weather observer said.

"Should we put on our ponchos?"

"If one does, we all have to."

"It's cold," the observer added.

"We can't wear them during the attack . . ."

. . . because you're trying to sneak up on the enemy while the ponchos are going slickety slickety.

"Hell, even if we wear them, we'll get wet."

"We are wet."

And cold. The Redlegs call it practicing to be miserable.

"We'll just have to roll them up again."

In the dark. Two hundred ponchos rolled to the same exact specifications.

"What's a little rain?"

"What's a lot of rain?"

"If we were smart enough to get out of the rain, we wouldn't be wearing the idiot sticks, would we?"

"Infantry!"

"Queen of Battles!"

"Follow ME!"

Mail call in the rain. (I received a letter from the Department of the Army. Had a mistake been made? Was I supposed to be a civilian? I stuck it unopened inside a sodden pocket.) Mess in the rain—pork chop soup.

Planning in the rain—we were supposed to write down our operations orders. The rain had pulped the paper, but we persevered. Assembly point. Line of departure. Line of assault. Guides. The guides learn the route, set up posts, and lead the attackers forward.

The rain poured down.

"Great," the instructor said. "Perfect weather for a night attack."

He was wearing a raincoat.

We attacked. The Aggressor Army ran away. The instructor critiqued us.

"Good job, men. Now let's get the hell out of the rain."

Onward, half-drowned soldiers.

Could it get any worse? Yes. The trucks assigned to us had no canvas tops and the wind was blowing and the rain was falling. We huddled in the backs of the trucks and shivered. Situation Normal—AFU. (But no matter how bad things are, they can always get worse.)

The trucks got lost. (The transportation officer who had gotten us lost was sitting in the comfortably warm, dry cab.) We roamed the reservation for two hours in search of a familiar landmark. The rain never stopped, nor the wind, until, at last, we spotted the jump towers and found the

BOQ. The trucks pulled up. An officer screamed maniacally, jumped off the truck, threw himself into a large puddle, and thrashed around. Then he stood up and we all went inside and cleaned our rifles.

While I was removing my sodden uniform I found the letter from the Department of the Army. Only the first line was legible:

WELCOME TO THE INFANTRY.

I dumped my uniform in the corner and flopped on the bed. This, I thought, is going to be a short night.

The next thing I knew I was standing in formation, fully clothed. I glanced at the person on my left. He disappeared. I glanced to the right. The whole formation evaporated. I must be dreaming . . . except I was standing at attention, fully clothed, alone in the middle of my room at three o'clock in the morning.

We were a tired and disgruntled group next day as we approached the bayonet training ground.

The spirit of the bayonet is ATTACK!

So the sergeant-instructors informed us, but then they told us to use sheathed blades, and, as we discovered, it is next to impossible to drive a sheathed blade into human flesh.

"Take it easy," the sergeant-instructors said.

They moved us on to the pugil sticks (poles the length of an M-14 with its bayonet fixed, padded at both ends); with them you are supposed to be able—safely—to practice thrusts, parries, and butt-strokes against a live opponent.

The two student officers selected as demonstrators had to be separated by a sergeant.

"Take it easy, gentlemen. It is possible to injure someone with these."

He chose a different pair of officers. They dropped the sticks and went after each other with bare hands. Four sergeants pulled them apart; the sergeants looked at us with wild surmise, but orders are orders, and they selected two more to go at it. One managed to get his thumbs on the other's throat before the sergeants intervened. A sergeant was knocked cold and the exercise was cancelled. ("These officers need no further instruction in the spirit of the bayonet.")

Bayonet drill was followed by a class on filling out forms.

"This is important, gentlemen, so listen up."

We dozed. One student fell asleep and off his chair and even then didn't wake up. Finally a brash soul raised his hand.

"Question?" the instructor asked (grateful for a sign of interest).

The student stood.

"Yes sir. Is it true, if we don't learn this, our dicks will drop off?"

The Ft. Benning Infantry Instructor had to be quick.

"No, lieutenant, that is not true. But you *will* die in Vietnam."

In the afternoon and evening we ran an exercise with the M-60 (machine gun). We waited for dark and a demonstration of final protective fire. To pass the time the instructor told us war stories.

"Every M-16 in the platoon jammed, but our M-60s fired all night long, even after the barrels burned out. I wouldn't be here, if . . ."

. . . if the M-60 were not as faithful as a shaggy dog.

When it was dark enough for tracers to leave a streak in the air, two M-60s began to fire, first in short bursts, then continuously, in interlocking lines of orange, until the barrels glowed, until the rifling burned out and the bullets tumbled. We stamped our feet and yelled.

"KILL! KILL! KILL!"

Area of Operations of the Twenty-Fifth Division

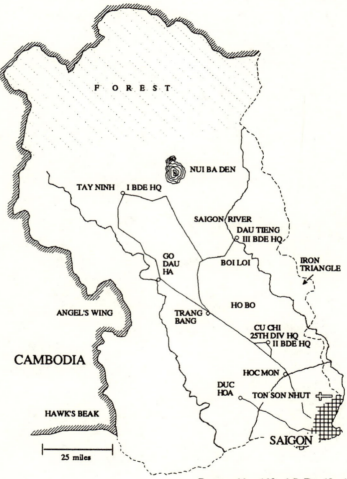

FOREST

NUI BA DEN

TAY NINH   I BDE HQ

SAIGON RIVER

DAU TIENG
III BDE HQ

GO
DAU
HA

BOI LOI

IRON
TRIANGLE

ANGEL'S WING

HO BO

TRANG
BANG

CU CHI
25TH DIV HQ
II BDE HQ

CAMBODIA

HOC MON

DUC
HOA

TON SON NHUT

HAWK'S BEAK

25 miles

SAIGON

Prepared by Alfred S. Bradford

Chapter 2

THE FIRST WOLFHOUNDS

While I was at Ft. Benning, the 1/27th Infantry (First Wolfhounds) was operating near Saigon out of the 25th Infantry Division Base at Cu Chi. The 1/27th Infantry with its sister battalion, the 2/27th (Second Wolfhounds), and the Fifth Mech (together known as the "Fire Brigade") had established the base.

The Wolfhounds were not heavily engaged in the '68 Tet offensive (though they had racked up a body count of four hundred in one battle), but they had their feet put to the fire in May and June. The survivors told me plenty about those days when I arrived in late September.

"The NVA assigned a regiment to follow us wherever we went . . . and destroy us. They almost succeeded," a lieutenant told me.

"We landed on an LZ. The CO and the Brigade CO were each circling overhead in their choppers. We were pinned down. I was crawling around on my face, trying to work my machine guns into position to give us some cover when I heard a chopper come down behind me. The next thing I know the CO is out in front of me with a .45 in his hand and he yells, 'Come on!' He charged at the tree line and we followed him."

(The Brigade Commander said, "That's the damnedest thing I've ever seen.")

"The CO could act like a crazy man, because the S-3 was as steady as Caesar."

A speedy-four told me, "I arrived in Nam one day and the next I was out with the Wolfhounds, in a bunker commanded by a PFC, and that night the NVA broke through the wire.

"I see these khaki-clad figures running at us and I look at them and Bennie [the bunker/squad leader] says to me, 'Shoot 'em,' and I say, 'Okay,' and I shoot, and some of them fall down and the rest run away and nobody seems very concerned about it and so I tell myself, okay, this is just another day in Vietnam, no sweat.

"The next day I meet my platoon leader. He's wearing a purple shirt, black shorts, and Ho Chi Minh sandals. He tells us the M-16 is a piece of junk and he's going to start carrying an AK-47. We say no way.

"We had contact practically every day. One day Bennie and I are walking point. He told me, 'If you're ever squad leader, you might as well walk in front, cuz if you take fire you have to come up and look anyway.'

"Well, we get into a bunker complex. The NVA let us get right next to the bunkers because they wanted to suck in the whole platoon. We were so close we were out of their field of fire. Suddenly, you know, bullets are coming out of the ground at our feet. We flop down. Everyone else thinks of course we've had it, and they're firing right at us, until they see Bennie drop a grenade through the firing slit of the bunker. The NVA keep on firing. Then an NVA pops up out of the ground and Bennie shoots him.

" 'Get going,' he tells me, so I think, yeah, okay, and I shoot the next NVA out of the hole. Bennie drops another grenade through the slit.

" 'Hey, you guys!' we hear.

"The platoon's calling to us.

" 'What?'

" 'Get back here!'

" 'You come up here!'

" 'No way. Get back here. We wanna call artillery.'

" 'No way!'

"But, you know, you keep plugging away, the company maneuvers, another company lands, and, suddenly, all the NVA are gone like ghosts.

"And you think, we've been at it twenty minutes maybe, and you check, and you've been there four hours."

"How come," I asked, "the grenades didn't knock out the bunker?"

"It was so jammed with NVA," he said, "that the frags didn't reach most of them."

By mid-summer this private had become a specialist-fourth-class ("speedy-four") and briefly, as the casualties mounted, a platoon leader.

"I wonder what I'm going to think about it all, when I'm a civilian again."

In June an ambush patrol ("Mustang 71A") had the following radio conversation with Operations ("Mustang 3").

"Mustang 3, this is Mustang 71A. Over."

"Mustang 71A, this is Mustang 3."

"This is Mustang 71A. We have made contact. Four victor charlie kilo, one victor charlie whiskey. Over."

". . . Mustang 3. Transmission error. Heard four victor charlie kilo, one victor charlie whiskey for five victor charlie kilo. Please advise. Over."

". . . Mustang 71A. Roger. Wait."

Pause.

". . . Mustang 71A. Affirmative. Five victor charlie kilo."

"And, Jesus," the RTO told me, "we had tied his arms and everything and after we shot him, we just left him like that till morning. Then, when the chopper was going to come in to get the bodies, we heard there might be a reporter, and we had to break his arms out of rigor mortis to make him look natural."

"That son of a gun of a platoon leader I had, we were told once we had to move at night and we could hear the NVA all around us and how the hell can you tell where you're going at night, so he had us walk two klicks down a stream bed. The Air Force was firing rockets all around us. We were directing them by radio. Then I fell flat on my face and the batteries got wet.

" 'Good move,' he said.

"I thought we'd had it then.

" 'What are we going to do?' I asked.

" 'You got it wet—you get us out of this.'

"He put a strobe in my tin pot and had me hold it up as high as I could reach and I had to walk twenty meters in front of the platoon. I was scared to a pinhead, but he got us out."

The Wolfhounds were assigned the peaceful little hamlet of Hoc Mon (about twenty-six miles northwest of Saigon). They built a fire support base there and relaxed, until, one night, an NVA regiment moved in.

"It was like a John Wayne movie," Lt. Brown (the S-5 when I knew him, but then a platoon leader) told me.

"It took us a week to cross the highway and the hootches didn't have one straw lying on top of another straw by the time we got across. We called in gunships and artillery. Jets dropped napalm so close that I lost my eyebrows. Our machine guns were laying down supporting fire. Green tracers were coming back at us. We'd get up and move forward and I'd hear myself yelling, 'Come on! Come on! Follow me!' And they'd lie down and you didn't always know whether they were dead, wounded, or just tired. Almost all the officers got it. Platoons were being led by speedy-fours. Took us a week to get across the highway."

At the end an enemy battalion was trapped inside the perimeter we threw around the town. The perimeter was so tight that our men couldn't fire their rifles for fear of hitting each other. APCs ran down and crushed

the NVA. Wolfhounds stacked up over two hundred bodies and left them
to rot in the ruins of the hamlet.

The S-5 said to the people, "Make your choice, VC or US."

Although the VC, and to a lesser extent the NVA, had taken fearsome
casualties from Tet and the May Offensive, they had achieved one objective—to shock the American public—and they had come close to a second objective—to wreck troop morale.

Under a new—the survivors said inept—commander, the Wolfhounds
lost their esprit. Among other incidents, a company was set down on an
occupied bunker complex.

"You haven't seen anything until you've seen an LZ filled with burning
choppers."

Practically the whole company became casualties. Men lost confidence
in the commander. Platoons of forty were down to ten, sometimes led by
PFCs, and the survivors were drinking beer, smoking dope, and going
crazy. Some would hold up their off-hand during a firefight—"It's a great
night to get hit." A few shot themselves in the foot. Others refused to
obey orders.

Discipline cracked. Some enlisted men—regulations allowed beer in
the field—would get reeling drunk and one—a meek and mild guy . . .
except after a couple of beers—tried to stab his company commander.
When I was adjutant I received a letter from his mother.

Dear Sir,

Sonny wrot me you put him in jail. I dont know what he done but he never
done nothin bad before. He is a good boy. If he done somthin bad its because of
whats done to him. This war changed him. He dint drink never. He dint drink
beer even. I dint want him to go to war. He is a good boy. Now you say he isnt
and you put him in jail. I want my boy back.

Worried Mother.

Another yelled at the Battalion commander.

"You goddamned murdering jackass!"

(The next day the CO had the private, now sober, paraded before him.

"You were drunk last night, weren't you, private?"

"Yes sir."

"Do you remember saying some things to me?"

"Yes sir. And I've got a few more things to say, too!")

A new regulation prohibited beer in the field.

The Wolfhound lieutenants earned their pay in the summer of '68.
They had to face down a mutiny every time they went out. Lt. Roger
Horn (known to his men as Roger Ram-Jet) got his troops together.

"No way we're going," his men said.

Lt. Horn would start out, radio handset in one hand, and the radio-telephone operator (RTO) would have to follow, the others would follow the RTO, and soon they would be in the boonies, still protesting.

These lieutenants kept the Battalion going—and as they kept the Wolfhounds going, so Infantry lieutenants throughout Vietnam held their units together. If the U.S. Army never came close to defeat in Vietnam, it is because of those young lieutenants, few of them career officers, who went through IOBC and OCS at Ft. Benning.

PART II

In the Rear

(September 1968)

Senator Hawk

Every twenty years or so, it seems,
Our Congressmen have patriotic dreams;
A vision of MacArthur, Grant, or Lee
Arises, beckons, orders, "Follow ME!"

The paths of glory lead to voting booths
When pols uphold the elemental truths
Of Motherhood, our Flag, the American Way.
THE GLORIOUS DEAD! We vow, someone will pay.

Will pay! O public money, of thee I sing,
And public oratory: "Let Freedom Ring . . .
Our Brave Young Men (both black and white—
In times like these, Americans unite) . . .
Our Boys in Service on Land and Sea,
Defending Free Elections. VOTE FOR ME!"

Chapter 3

OUT OF THE WORLD

As we approached the U.S. Air Force Base at Bien Hoa the captain announced, "We are now beginning our final descent. The ground temperature is ninety-nine degrees. The ceiling is one thousand feet. Rain is predicted. Rocket fire is light to moderate."

Then we came down like gangbusters and our stomachs flopped.

So this is it.

I expected the war to begin at the foot of the off-ramp, but we left the plane without incident, marched across the air strip, and clambered onboard an ancient—and much scarred—bus, its windows cross-hatched with wire and its door, once we were inside, blocked by an armed guard. The wire was there to stop grenades, I suppose; the guard (I'm sure some among us thought) was there to keep those inside the bus inside the bus.

We passed a hollywood papa-san wearing a straw hat and driving a water buffalo. Camera shutters clicked. A helicopter flew over the bus and we stared wide-eyed like rubes in the big city. Costume, props, special effects, I could have been on the set of *The Green Berets*, except there were no pyrotechnics.

LBJ (Long Binh Junction to us, Long Binh Jail to some) was one of two transit centers in the south (for the in-coming, the out-going, and the Resting & Recuperating). We were escorted to a barracks jammed wall-to-wall and floor-to-ceiling with bunk bed frames and mildewed mattresses.

A talkative guide—and guard—showed us around.

"During Tet . . . a few months ago . . . a VC . . . my friend told me this . . . crawled up along that ditch there all the way into the compound and one of the guards shot him right at that spot where I'm pointing."

We looked at him with respect; after all, he had known the man who knew the guard who shot the VC . . . and we could all see the ditch.

The next day I was flown to Cu Chi, the division base of the 25th Infantry Division, driven to the reppo-deppo (a large quonset hut), and given forms to fill out:

Name:
Rank:
Serial Number:
Social security number:
Distinguishing marks:
Next of kin:
If you receive a wound for which you are awarded a Purple Heart, but for which you are not hospitalized or sent out-of-country, do you wish NOK to be notified?

"Hell, yes," a lieutenant said. "Why shouldn't my wife worry a little?"

"Is that what Nok means?" a private asked (confusing the term, no doubt, with nookie). "What do I do? I don't have a Nok."

Division reppo-deppo assigned me to the Second Brigade and I was driven to its HQ—more paper work—and reassigned to the 1/27th Infantry ("They've lost a lot of officers lately."); the Battalion adjutant was notified and I waited for him outside. While I was waiting, I noticed a sad-sack officer standing near me—an emaciated, bandaged lieutenant with a bad case of the jerks and . . . I knew him.

"Hey, lieutenant!"

He stared at me.

"Remember me? IOBC Four? How's it going?"

"I've been here two months," he said.

I waited for him to say more, but he just stood there, stared at the ground, and shuffled his feet.

"Yes . . . and what've you been up to?"

"I've been out there."

"So what's it like?"

"Christ."

"You're wounded."

"Twice."

"How'd it happen?"

"I have to go back out."

A jeep beeped. The adjutant.

"Well, so long. Good luck."

On the way to Battalion we passed a couple of armed guards watching three slight men in black pajamas. The three slight men appeared depressed.

"That's the enemy?" I asked.

"Yup," the adjutant replied.

My face must have given my thoughts away—they don't look so tough—because he added, "They're a lot bigger when they're armed."

He took me to the Battalion Officers Club and introduced me around. The Surgeon. Captain Crux (the chaplain). Major Lynch, the executive officer (XO). Lt. Brown, the S-5 (civic action). Two new infantry lieutenants.

"Howdy, howdy, howdy."

The club had a bar, a small stage, stools, and a little pile of scrap lumber left over from the last rocket attack.

"Have a drink," the XO said. "Have two. And how about you, Padre? Don't you owe me one?"

"I guess maybe I do," the chaplain said, "but I can't buy you liquor." He was a Baptist.

"I'll have a beer, then."

The chaplain shook his head.

"I couldn't pay for alcohol. Why, when I was courting," he said, "I took my wife . . . course she wasn't my wife then . . . to a dance . . . course we didn't dance . . . and my wife said to me, 'Would you try to stop me, if I wanted to buy a beer?' And I said, 'Well, I guess I couldn't stop you, but I certainly wouldn't respect you any more.'"

"Okay," the XO said, "You're not getting off the hook. I'll have a 7-Up."

Other officers drifted in. After a while the adjutant rapped his glass on the bar.

"We seem to have a quorum. Shall we initiate the new officers? Bartender, mix them the Wolfhounder."

The bartender mixed the Wolfhounder—as far as I could tell, a shot from every bottle on the bar, tossed in a waterglass, no ice—and we were expected to chug it down (and not chug it back up). The chaplain departed. I drank the drink and then I moved to a corner to sit where I could have two walls to lean against as I listened to the buzz.

After a while I heard a voice say, "The puking buzzards."

I thought the phrase was being applied (aptly enough) to the two new Infantry lieutenants, but no—a gang of officers with eagles (agape) upon their shoulders had just entered the bar.

"We're going to clean this place out," their leader announced.

I didn't even know these guys. I slid to the floor and—except for an occasional, involuntary, blink of the eyes—played possum.

Blink. The XO was down with a boot in his face. A chair was travelling slowly across the room, suspended in mid-air. Blink. The adjutant had a hammerlock on a blond head. BAM! He rammed it against the bar. Blink. The new lieutenants were lying in a pool of beer and Wolfhounder. Blink. An MP lieutenant was in the room and he was demanding names. Should I rise? Blink. The MP lieutenant was face down—limp. Blink. An enlisted cop was biting a chunk out of the stage. Blink. The XO kicked him in the back of the head. Blink. Teeth tinkled to the floor.

On the morning of 8 October 1968 a much subdued officer replacement rode the convoy out to the fire support base to meet his new CO. I locked and loaded. The ride took about an hour—we had to wait for a truck to catch up, had to stop at Alpha Company (which was securing Hoc Mon bridge), and, everytime we stopped, Vietnamese children and girls flocked around to sell us cold beer, food, watches, clothes, Coke and themselves. Their English was fluent.

"Hey, G.I., you want Coke?"

"You souvenir me one time, baby-san?"

"Souvenir? Souvenir my ass."

The Battalion fire support base was located near the peaceful little hamlet of Hoc Mon, a hamlet so peaceful, in fact, that G.I.'s thought they could go for a stroll unarmed, drink a beer, nod at the papa-sans, consort with the Coke-girls, and talk with the kids. This was the hamlet that had been destroyed, straw by straw.

I saw my first for-real combat patrol setting out: The troops wore dark glasses, purple scarves, sandals, they carried their weapons casually propped over a shoulder, and they were conversing—a nice day for a walk.

"If we didn't mother-hen 'em," the platoon leader said, "they'd go out with the load in their piece and zip else."

The Battalion CO, Lt. Colonel Mark L. Reese, Jr., appointed me S-1 (adjutant) and told me his philosophy.

"No worthwhile mission is impossible."

Chapter 4

THE RUFF-PUFFS HAVE A PARTY

We were expected to cooperate with the local forces, called collectively the Regional Force and Provincial Force, with the acronym RF-PF, thus Ruff-Puffs. A medic, who had accompanied the Ruff-Puffs, an adviser sergeant, and a reinforced U.S. squad on an operation, told me this story.

We're sent out [the medic said] with the Ruff-Puffs: Me, a doofus sergeant from Germany who thinks he knows everything, and a reinforced squad. At least we have an M-60 and a radio.

I take one look at the Ruff-Puffs and I know we're in trouble. Frankly, I'd rather go out with the National Guard.

So, anyway, we're lifted out to this village and we have to walk through a melon patch and the Ruff-Puffs are eating melons and smashing the ones they don't eat and diddling around and I'm saying, I hope these bastards get blown away, and then I think, hey, it's my butt, too, and the doofus sergeant's got his head up it, so I say to Georgie [the squad leader], let's get a little distance here, and he starts to walk slow and the Ruff-Puffs get ahead and then we lie down and let the Ruff-Puffs go and the Lifer's saying we have to keep up, we can't get left, and nobody's paying any attention.

So they get into the village and it's okay and we follow them and they're taking every chicken that isn't nailed down, and they say, "VC! VC! All VC!"

And the Ruff-Puff honcho slaps an old man around and they're all hassling the broads and I figure we're going to have a rape or two, and I tell the Lifer to get the Ruff-Puffs to stop it.

"It's none of our business," the Lifer says. "Let them handle their own people."

He doesn't have orders, you know, so Georgie goes to the edge of the village and we set up there. And then we have to walk to another village and by now even the Lifer knows enough to let the Ruff-Puffs go first.

And sure enough we draw fire—maybe one AK, a couple carbines—and the gooks are screaming and running and firing everywhere—they're more dangerous than charlie and I figure it's gonna be a massacre except we lay down some M-60 and Georgie sees the bunker and we maneuver and a grunt shoves in a grenade and that's all she wrote.

Half those Ruff-Puffs are running yet, I bet, but the rest, they see we've got it under control and they come up and jump around like monkeys and then we hear groans coming from the bunker and they shoot off their rifles and start jabbering and Georgie says screw it and he goes in and he begins to hand out bodies only we must have greased a medical group because it's VC nurses except for one poor enemy grunt and he's had it, of course, and so have they, only there's one that has a frag wound in the upper chest, so I take a look at her, while the Arvn officer is jabbering.

"You do! You do!"

And I figure she may make it so I bandage her. Anyway, I finish and he pulls her pants off and he rapes her and she screams and his men—maybe there're a hundred of them—line up and take a turn.

"We don't want no part of this," the Lifer says and he walks away.

"Walking away from it is just as bad as doing it yourself," I tell him.

"Just shut up," the Lifer says.

Meanwhile she stops screaming and they're still putting it to her. I go over and take a look. She's dead, but that don't stop them.

We're supposed to spend the night with the Ruff-Puffs and the Lifer is going to lead us into their compound.

"No way," Georgie says.

We set up a perimeter outside the road. This daiwi [Arvn captain] comes around.

"Beaucoup VC! Beaucoup!" he says. "You shoot. VC beaucoup smart. VC maybe same-same Arvn. Uniform same-same Arvn. VC smart. We smart. We same-same this."

He rolls one sleeve up and the other one down.

"All Arvn same-same. You see no same-same, you kekedau."

Right.

So we're laagered there and we're kinda hanging, you know, and the Lifer is nervous because he thinks we'd be better off with the Ruff-Puffs and then here comes a jeep and there're four gooks in it and they have both their sleeves rolled up to their ears and the Lifer says,

"VC!"

And we say, naw, dumb gooks, and he says, VC! and we say, it's just that ten percent, and he's getting all worked up because that Arvn tells us about the smart VC and the jeep is up to us and the Lifer is going ape so Georgie says, okay, already, and he blows the driver away and we grease the rest.

Then it's dark and Georgie stands up and moves out and we follow him and the Lifer is whispering, hold it, where are you going, only we don't say diddly, but we move and sure enough, a couple hours later, blam, gook mortars hit our last position.

["Well," I asked, "were the gooks in the jeep Arvns?"
"Of course they were," the medic said.]

We wrote a little song called "The Episode."

> Dead nurses in a bunker,
> Lying in a row.
> Did any of them wiggle?
> Did that one move a toe?
>
> The daiwi calls our medic,
> "Come to help her quick.
> Come, come to bandage up her
> And then I dip my wick."
>
> The little VC nurses,
> Lying in a row,
> Surrounded by the Arvns,
> Do their mothers know?
>
> Our medic tells the daiwi,
> "I think she's almost done."
> The daiwi tells the medic,
> "I spike her with my gun."
>
> A hundred hungry Arvns,
> Standing in a row,
> All waiting for the warm one.
> "Regards to Uncle Ho!"

1/27th (First Wolfhounds) Area of Operations

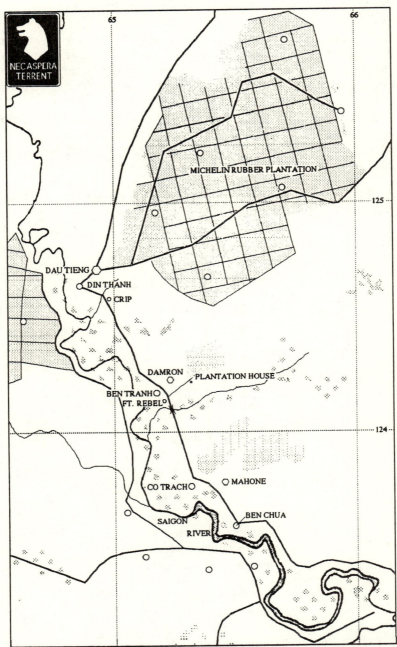

NEC ASPERA TERRENT

MICHELIN RUBBER PLANTATION

125

DAU TIENG

DIN THÁNH

CRIP

DAMRON

PLANTATION HOUSE

BEN TRANH

FT. REBEL

124

CO TRACH

MAHONE

BEN CHUA

SAIGON

RIVER

65

66

Prepared by Alfred S. Bradford

PART III

Dau Tieng

(1 October–19 November 1968)

Phuoc Thieu Tu

When day has gone to beddy-bye
And stars and moon have climbed the sky,
We sometimes hear an alien cry,
"Phuoc ieu, phuoc ieu."

The forward bunker pops a flare
And into its flickering light we stare . . .
And stare and stare, but no one's there.
"Phuoc ieu, phuoc ieu."

Is it a magical yellow-skinned wizard?
An invisible priest who'll cut out our gizzard?
Not in the least, it's merely a beast:
The famous incredible Phuoc Ieu Lizard.

Such a beast is no surprise—
From the mountains to the beaches,
From the peasants to the leaches,
Nothing likes G.I.'s.

Such a beast is no surprise,
For it's the voice of Nam you hear,
That lizard calling in your ear,
"Phuoc ieu! Phuoc ieu!"

Chapter 5

DEMOCRACY IN ACTION

Colonel Reese ("No worthwhile mission is impossible.") was just the man to bring back the Wolfhounds, and in the end he did, but both he and the Battalion went through hell to do it, because the Wolfhounds were snakebit.

A patrol returned from an entire, cold (75–80 degrees), empty night on ambush and huddled for warmth around a burning trash barrel. The barrel exploded. The explosion blew an arm and both legs off a sergeant. (He lived two days.) A flying piece of metal punched a hole through another man's chest. The blast brought the surgeon and his medics on the run; the surgeon immediately started working on the chest wound.

"It's okay, son."

The blood bubbled and frothed with every breath the wounded man took, but human beings are tough and often hard to kill, unless they go into shock. A man can die from a nick in the arm, if he convinces himself he's had it and he panics. *I'm going to die.* His veins collapse, he dies. In this case, however, with the doctor right there, calm and efficient, reassuring him, the wounded man had no reason to go into shock, no reason at all, until the chaplain kneeled beside him and said, "Shall we pray, my son?"

"I'm dying!" the wounded man cried.

The doctor knocked the chaplain aside.

"You dumb son of a bitch! Hell no, son, you're not dying. A month from now you'll be chugging sake and chasing geisha girls all over Tokyo."

The soldier was stable when the dust-off arrived. After the dust-off, the chaplain came to the doctor to receive an apology and to deliver a sermon on the text of the exploding trash barrel.

"They think that someone put a 4.2-inch mortar round in the barrel. I've been warning soldiers to be careful and they haven't paid any attention. Maybe now they'll listen."

The doctor was a bit ashamed of himself and so he refrained from putting a name to the chaplain's sermon, but Captain Crux's sheep began to stray and those who remained apologized to the rest of us.

"I don't like him any better than you do, but he's the only game in town."

The exploding trash barrel was the worst in a series of bad accidents, accidents which the Battalion seemed unable to shake, though otherwise the Wolfhounds of Colonel Reese were walking proud. When they saluted, they said, "First Wolfhounds, sir!" (Saluted officers of other units commented, "What in the hell are you supposed to reply: 'Don't bend over?' ")

Colonel Reese brought enlisted men into staff meetings so they would understand the current operation, and he took them up in the air with him, so they could see what he did. He wrote letters to their homes, just to say that they were doing a great job. He espoused a simple philosophy, "Mission, men, me," and perhaps he even went farther and put the men first. "Take care of the men and the mission will take care of itself." Officers, however, are not "men." We sweated.

On 13 October 1968 Division sent elements of the First Wolfhounds northwest from Cu Chi about forty-five kilometers to Nui Bau Dinh (The Black Virgin Mountain). Division Intelligence had received a report that the NVA were going to try to knock over Tay Ninh. Division ordered the Wolfhounds to block the northern approaches around Nui Bau Dinh with platoon-sized elements. The mission was also designed to test the progress LTC Reese had made with the Battalion.

Which was all very well, but . . .

"What are we supposed to do," a lieutenant asked, "if an NVA division does come?"

"Give them a road map."

"Salute and say, 'First Wolfhounds, sir!' "

"Hunker down. In June I was on ambush. NVA walked into our killzone. We waited to hit 'em in the rear. We lay there and waited . . . and waited . . . and waited . . . and they kept coming through. An NVA division. My men were scared that I was crazy enough to pop it on a division."

The attack on Tay Ninh did not materialize, but the Battalion (Division decided) was battle-ready, and so we received a reward. Our reward was Dau Tieng. The Dau Tieng area (about twenty-six miles northwest of

Saigon) consisted of forest, rice paddy, and . . . The Michelin Rubber Plantation.

The First Wolfhounds were familiar with Dau Tieng and the Michelin. In November 1966 we had helped establish a base at Dau Tieng for the Third Brigade of the 25th Infantry Division.

The Michelin was the NVA's happy hunting ground. Whenever American troops went there, the NVA shot at us and we shot at them. In the process rubber trees were damaged. Rumor had it that for every damaged rubber tree we had to reimburse de Gaulle a hundred smackers . . . and he was the one who counted the trees. Furthermore, we asked, how could rubber be harvested (for sale to the West) in an NVA-dominated area?

Our mission was, break the NVA hold on the Dau Tieng and Michelin area. Three hamlets (Ben Tranh, Co Trach, and Ben Chua) south of Dau Tieng were VC rest areas. Division proposed that our Battalion climb on helicopters, pounce upon Co Trach (which was supposed to have a population of about five hundred), and kill or capture every man or woman between the ages of fourteen and forty-five. Agents had a blacklist with the code names of VC leaders.

The mission was timed to begin with the end of the rainy season. The timing was precise. As we stood down on 21 and 22 October and refitted in Tay Ninh, the heavens released the last storm of the rainy season—a violent, two-hour downpour, an hour of sun and steam, and then a violent three-hour downpour. In the midst of the preparations and the weather, MAC-V decreed C-day.

The United States government, in an effort to control currency speculation and the black market, issued script called MPC instead of greenback currency. The Vietnamese who earned MPC legitimately could exchange it for their own currency (piasters), but not for gold or for American dollars, and they were not supposed to hold MPC for more than a few days, and certainly they were not supposed to accumulate it.

Periodically, then, on a single day (C-day), all the old script was called in and new script was issued, dollar for dollar. On C-day any Vietnamese who could not show he had reason to possess the MPC he had, or who had more than he was supposed to have, could not exchange it, and so found himself stuck with worthless scraps of paper. (G.I.'s, too, had to account for holdings of more than a couple of hundred dollars.)

Frantic Vietnamese implored G.I.'s to exchange their script for them, fifty cents on the dollar. Some G.I.'s did exchange it and hopped a chopper to the field with a small fortune in their pockets.

There once was a MAC-V lieutenant, so the story goes, who brought some monopoly money with him to Vietnam in hopes he would be in-country for C-day. Lo and behold, he was. And he convinced the indigenous marketeers that his monopoly money was freshly printed script. They begged him and they bribed him—he had to take his ten percent so they wouldn't suspect his motives—and finally he agreed to exchange their old, supposedly worthless MPC, dollar for monopoly dollar (minus ten percent).

All I could say was, thank the Lord C-day came when we were on stand-down and not in the field. I had to send authorized agents back to Cu Chi to pick up the necessary forms (every dollar to the last cent had to be recorded), and then exchange the whole Battalion's script, but I did not have to go to ambush sites and platoon posts, company laagers, and a fire support base. We completed the exchange at noon on the 22nd.

On Wednesday 23 October we moved by convoy from Tay Ninh to Dau Tieng. Our parent unit was still the Second Brigade, but we had been detached to the Third; our move was so secret that the staff of Second Brigade Headquarters did not know we had moved, and, in Dau Tieng, men kept stopping in at our new HQ:

"What unit is this?"

"First of the Twenty-Seventh."

"The Wolfhounds?"

"That's a rog."

"Are all of you here?"

"Sure are."

"Well, I'll be damned."

The NVA regiment stationed in the Dau Tieng area was tough, and the NVA were prepared to fight—in two preliminary brushes with them in a two-day period twenty-three Americans had been killed, so we tried to catch them unprepared.

Arvn troops did not operate in the Tri Tam District. The District Chief commanded the 170th RF-PF "Ruff-Puffs." The Ruff-Puffs had their own compound, which nestled as close as they could get to the Third Brigade base. They were under-manned, poorly equipped, and poorly paid. Their morale was shot. They went along with us.

At seven A.M. on 24 October 1968 our blocking forces moved out—thirty slicks, with 96 Americans and 60–70 Ruff-Puffs, in the air at the same time. Our forces quickly surrounded the hamlet of Co Trach; one company swept up as many people as possible and another searched the area hootch by hootch. Co Trach's population of 500 turned out to be more than 1100.

The villagers knew of Americans only what they had been told by the NVA: We would shoot the men, rape the women, and drink the blood of the innocent children. (But the NVA—heroic defenders of the people—

would stop us. Americans are paper tigers.) That's what the NVA said, but they beat it into the bush and left the people to their fate.

The people were sullen and suspicious. They expected the old roust-and-requisition, Arvn-style, which probably would be interrupted by fragments of steel . . . and they didn't like the looks of the pole the engineers were erecting. Before the day was over someone would be swinging from the top or the NVA didn't know Americans.

We were no less suspicious of them.

"Notice how there aren't any young men," the Battalion CO said.

The people we had collected were women, children, and elderly men, then faceless, though soon we would get to know them . . . one old man in particular. The young men, who were not there, were all VC except for the few the Arvns had nabbed.

Our troops stared at the natives and the natives stared back. Nobody moved. Then Lopez, a medic assigned to S-5, waved at a little girl and she waved back. He held out a piece of candy and motioned to her to come get it and, before the horrified parents could grab her, she darted out.

"G.I.! G.I.!" she said.

Lopez gave her the candy and she scurried back to her parents. They scolded her, but the crowd seemed to relax a bit. Perhaps we wouldn't drink blood after all. Lt. Brown, the S-5, gave out candy and RVN T-shirts; the T-shirts were colored like the flag, yellow with three red stripes (appropriate, we said: The part of Vietnam that's not red is yellow).

That night (we hoped) Nguyen van Rouge, local VC, after a hard day in the boonies dodging HE, willy-peter, mini-guns, and the other implements of American foreign policy, returned home to relax in the bosom of his family and see his little Nguyen. What did you do today, Little Nguyen? A new shirt? Trot it out. Kajua! Running dog imperialist! Take that!

The children became our first converts. Lt. Brown trained them (for candy) to line the convoy route and chant,

"Woof'ouns! Woof'ouns!"

We turned them into stoolies.

When will your daddy be home?

Tonight.

Well, we'll just have to arrange a party.

Our real target, of course, was the adult population, to win them over with promises of freedom and democracy; as a first sample of democracy-in-action we held an election for hamlet chiefs and village chief. The chiefs-elect would be sent off to Arvn school to learn to politick.

Volunteers?

No one moved. No one spoke.

"Look at those poor suckers sweat."

No one wanted to be the goat. The District Chief consulted his MAC-V adviser, the adviser advised, the District Chief nodded, examined the crowd, and conducted the election Arvn style: I want five candidates—you, you, you, you, and you!

An open covenant, openly arrived at,
And free elections, nothing connived at.

Thus five men from the village were sentenced to death (with a limited stay of execution). They gasped, blanched, and were immediately deserted by their friends and neighbors. We bunched the five in a cluster at the foot of the flag pole, hoisted the flag and—Smile!—they were photographed.

"Do the little bastards have an anthem?"

Chapter 6

CONVOY

The first day of the mission, while we were establishing our perimeter, Captain Ervin (of "C" Company) was sitting on a bunker in a bunker complex of unknown extent. He could hear sporadic small arms fire, and he wondered just how many enemy there might be in the immediate area. He was feeling lonely . . . lonely, isolated, and exposed.

He asked his Arvn aide, "You think beaucoup VC?"

"No, daiwi . . . ," the Arvn replied and Captain Ervin was relieved. "No beaucoup VC . . . beaucoup NVA."

The NVA, however, did not engage in force and by nightfall the Wolfhounds had sent 116 detainees and 25 VC to Dau Tieng. No Americans had been killed, though three had been wounded, one from "C" Company, the others from chopper crews.

The Battalion set up a fire support base (FSB Mahone) at Co Trach. The S-4 (Captain Wong) was kept busy ferrying in sandbags and concertina wire . . . and more concertina. Snipers fired across the wire all night. An ambush patrol made heavy contact and three more wounded were brought in.

Meanwhile I was at a desk in an old French plantation house with parquet floors, cream-colored walls, and a red tile roof. I had spent the day shuffling papers and listening to the XO harangue the administrative sergeant about dirt and dust in the building. The XO loved the floors and he had declared war on dust.

In the evening I eavesdropped on the Battalion radio net; I heard the dust-off called for the ambush and a short time later a lieutenant appeared with a bandage around his head. He didn't look at all like John Wayne or Randolph Scott. He looked like anybody, but he had an air about him—call it self-possession—as he squatted on the floor (the floor

the XO loved), removed a can of C-rations from one pocket, a chunk of
C-4 from another, rolled the C-4 around the can, and set it on fire.

"Goddammit," the XO hollered at him. "This isn't a barn."

The lieutenant paid no attention to him.

"We were on our way to the ambush site," he said, "when we took fire.
The gooks were in spider holes in the tree line. We had to crawl up on
them. One of my men reached into a hole and caught a gook by the hair
and pulled him out and cut his throat. I dropped a grenade down the
hole. Another gook tried to throw it back. He almost made it."

He shoved a hunk of half-burned spaghetti into his mouth.

"That's how I got it," he said. "But you should see the gook."

We had caught the NVA by surprise. They abandoned the villagers and
we used their absence to blitz the hamlets with civic action. Civic action
was then in its good works phase—we bring you food, clothing, medicine
—and we convinced the inhabitants of Co Trach that it was in their
interest to profess friendliness, at least; the inhabitants of another hamlet
were not so receptive. The medcap teams had to fight their way in, secure
a perimeter, treat the villagers at gunpoint, and fight their way out. Even
the children were hostile—they refused candy—and so the order came
down to the recon platoon: Convert the natives.

"Roger, sir," said the recon platoon leader, Lt. Davis. He was a magi-
cian. He (and his men) visited the hamlet and the hamlet disappeared in
a puff of smoke. (The villagers moved closer to our fire support base,
where we could "secure" them.)

We had shown the villagers that the NVA could not keep us out, but
we had yet to prove that we could stay. Resupply by air drained Division's resources, and once Division had decided that our mission would
be extended beyond a few days, the decision was also made to attempt to
resupply us by road. The road from Dau Tieng to Co Trach was closed.
For two years it had been closed. For two years no friendly vehicle had
been down that road. Division ordered the Wolfhounds to open that
road, no matter what the cost, and the NVA declared that our convoys
would not get through. They put their prestige on the line.

The first company to clear the road fought all the way from Dau Tieng
to Mahone and all the way back, and the next day the next company
fought all the way from wire to wire, and the next, and every day after
that, for weeks.

We established a strong point at the bridge at Ben Tranh. The NVA
shot at the company and they mortared the strong point. They mined the
road and they ambushed it. They shot RPGs at our vehicles . . . and
AKs and RPDs and whatever else they had in their arsenal.

Captain Ervin described (à la Bill Cosby) his first stroll down the road to Fire Support Base Mahone.

"We flipped a coin. The ref said call it. 'Heads,' I said. It's tails. So Charlie chooses lying-in-the-bushes-and-shooting-at-us-from-cover and we walk right down the middle of the road."

"Anyone get hit?" I asked.

"Naw. That'd be unnecessary roughness."

For ten years, so went the story, no good guy had travelled the road and lived to tell the tale.

"I want to know one thing," Captain Ervin said. "Who clears the road for us?"

More men were scared than hurt, but plenty were hurt and they kept finding mines; one day they found—as the operator of the mine detector kept repeating—a mine "bigger than me," with wires running off into the brush. They followed the wires, the wires ran to a spider hole, the spider hole was empty . . . except for a detonator. Out of curiosity, and because the NVA booby-trap their booby traps (so that it is not a good idea to try to disarm a mine), the troops set off the detonator. The mine was live and in good working order.

"If Charlie hadn't been on his coffee break . . ."

After security reported that the road was "secure," the convoy set out. The S-4 (supply), Captain Wong, and the transportation lieutenant alternated runs as convoy commander. Captain Wong's runs were, comparatively speaking, smooth and quiet; the lieutenant's . . . well . . . his nickname was Magnet.

"The captain taking us out today?" a relatively composed troop would ask.

"Nope. Magnet."

(The lieutenant had received three purple hearts in three months.)

"Magnet? Jeez! Where'd I put my flak jacket?"

I rode the convoy, when I could, because I had not come all the way to Vietnam to miss the action, and the convoy was the only game available to me. Before I went I looked for our Engineer lieutenant.

Due to the unavailability of Infantry lieutenants, the Army was now assigning other branches as staff to Infantry battalions. One of the officers was Lt. James Artman, a patrician as a civilian (an architect who had sold his first hundred thousand dollar house before he was drafted) and as an officer (Engineers). He went through basic training and OCS and found his way, somehow, to the 1/27th.

"Hey, Lt. Artman, want to go along for the ride?"

"No, thank you. Unlike the Infantry, the Engineers don't take courses in stupidity."

I rode out with Captain Wong.

"The corn is on the way. ETA 1330."

The captain put me and a radio in the last vehicle.

"Charlie charlie, hotel romeo? Over."

"Lima charlie. Hotel mike? Over."

"Same-same water buffalo. The corn is on the way. We'll drop the tango at the bravo. Over."

"Roger. Shall we leave the victor with the mike there? Over."

"Affirm. We'll catch it on the rebound. Out." (Translation: "C[ommunications] c[heck]. H[ow do you] r[ead me]? Over." "L[oud and] c[lear]. H[ow do you read] m[e]? Over." "The same. The convoy is on the way. We'll drop the t[railer] at the b[ridge]. Over." "Okay. Shall we leave the v[ehicle] with the m[ail] there? Over.")

The road had been swept; maybe the mine was installed after the sweep went by, because the truck in front of me rose into the air—I saw it rise, saw the flash, heard the explosion—and still didn't comprehend.

What has four wheels and flies?

I give up. What?

A truck that's hit a mine!

Hey, that could have been me!

Before the truck ceased rocking the driver was out with his hands to his face.

"Damn it! I knew it! I knew it! Damn it! I knew I was too short to drive a truck. I knew this was going to happen."

Metal shards, as thin as thread, had been blown into his eyes, though none had punctured the eyeball. For a month he wept metal.

(Bravo Company [Captain Rubino] did catch the VC who blew up the three-quarter. The VC was blindfolded, put in a huey, and flown back to Dau Tieng. As the huey was coming in to land, hovering a foot off the ground at full rotation, the HHC commandant Roger Ram-Jet kicked him out.)

The rest of the convoy run was uneventful. A VC did shoot at us with a carbine, but he missed, and, anyway, the infantryman's prayer is, if I get hit, let it be with a carbine (small hole in, small hole out).

I stayed at the fire support base, got the gossip, and wrote up a few citations.

Before the convoy left on its return, the convoy commander was told that all the villagers in a nearby hamlet, through which the road ran, had fled after locking their doors. We were tense, but no ambush developed.

I returned safely to my desk and found the following letter:

Dear Murderers,

You wrote that my son was shot. If he was shot why was the coffin sealed? What are you hiding? You sit in your office and you send my son out to die and then you lie about it.

I received his effects. Where is his driver's license? He always carried his driver's license and it isn't among his effects. How much did they pay for an American driver's license?

And we sent him a box of cookies weeks ago and he never received them and it was sent back to us and it looks like rats chewed on it.

I hope you can sleep nights.

Grieving Mother.

Her son had been half of a two-man point on a platoon patrol during the rainy season. The platoon was ambushed. He was shot and killed. The other man was wounded, but he managed to crawl to safety. The platoon traded fire with the NVA, the enemy gained fire superiority, and the platoon was forced to withdraw so the company killer could call in artillery. The firefight continued all night. So did the rain. So did the artillery. The next day the company advanced and recovered the body, but the body had lain in no man's land all night—it had been hit repeatedly by bullets and by fragments from grenades and shells and it was sodden with rain, hardly distinguishable from the mud it lay in. The papers on the body had been churned into a bloody pulp. We put the body in a closed casket and sent it and the effects (but not the bloody pulp) home. The platoon leader wrote a letter to the parents, describing how their son had been killed, but from kindness he spared them a description of what the body had suffered after death.

Why did the soldier's mother rip into us? We didn't want her son to die. An Infantry lieutenant's proudest boast was, "I didn't send anyone home in a bag."

"She's got to blame someone," Lt. Artman said.

"Well, then, let her blame those murdering bastards in Congress."

On 31 October the Battalion found a hospital and an ammunition factory with over seven hundred grenades in stock. Both were destroyed. A hamlet burned down.

In the first week of the operation the 1/27th killed forty-five VC/NVA, captured more than two hundred suspects, and destroyed tons of equipment and food.

Chapter 7

PACIFICATION

On 1 November the Wolfhounds ran wild. They stormed through the area and captured all kinds of equipment—mortar rounds, an RPD, hospital gear. Above them hung a pall of smoke and the Battalion commander raged over the phone.

"Don't burn the villages! Don't burn the villages!"

"Roger, One," a matter-of-fact voice replied. "Heat lightning is very prevalent out here."

Our morale was up. NVA morale was down. Rumors flew. The NVA were massing for an attack. Two battalions. Two regiments. Two divisions. On 4 November Division Intelligence reported that the NVA were assembling forces to knock over Dau Tieng. I—the XO was on R&R—was invited to Brigade to hear the news. Staff adrenalin was flowing and so were staff jitters. For the first time I realized what a monster their imaginations had made out of the NVA.

He could do anything. He could sneak up on an American and snip the buttons off his jungle fatigues. He could break through any barrier. He could mass any number of men. He never ran short of supplies. He could live on a handful of rice and a scoop of muddy water. He never got sick. No matter how many NVA we killed—if we could kill any—more would come. He was invulnerable.

I was not impressed with the Brigade staff. I returned to our area, called in the officers, talked over the situation, heard their suggestions, and then I went to bed.

The NVA did not come that night.

That same night Captain [soon Major] Cox of "D" Company (once called by the Division commander "the finest rifle company in Vietnam") was on ambush near Ben Tranh.

"Sir," one of his men whispered, "there's movement in the village."

Captain Cox had heard the intelligence report and, for all he knew, the movement in the hamlet was an NVA division, but he lived by the maxim "do to them before they do to you," and he had never been impressed by the rules of engagement handed down from on high. He ordered his mortars to fire a few rounds. The mortars set a hootch on fire. The fire spread. Captain Cox heard the Vietnamese yell as they fled from the fire; some were trapped in the flames . . . and they screamed.

"Oh, oh," he thought, "I'm in big trouble," and then one of the burning hootches exploded—grenades, rockets, mortars—all stockpiled by the VC for the NVA.

"I have to admit," he told me, "I was relieved to see that hootch go up."

Lt. Cleveland (a platoon leader) was not there—he had been detailed as pay officer.

"Damn!" he said. "They're burning hootches and I'm in the rear."

The pay officer goes to the rear, collects and counts the payroll, and then he delivers it. Even in the midst of a battle, the troops get paid. The pay officer may have to crawl on his belly in the mud through shot and shell from foxhole to foxhole, but the troops get paid.

"I'd almost rather burn a hootch than pop an ambush," Lt. Cleveland said.

"How's it going out there?" I asked.

"We've got them on the run."

The Wolfhounds were having a spectacular success, but even as the hootches packed with NVA ordnance exploded, the Wolfhound hoodoo was still claiming victims. A private tried to set a claymore off; when it didn't explode he removed the detonator. The detonator blew up in his hand. Another private was going to throw a stick of C-4 off the bridge near Ben Tranh to see if dead fish would rise to the surface. He lit the fuse.

"Throw it, man," someone said.

"Mind your own business," he replied. "I know what I'm . . ."

BAM!

It blew his head off.

Two of our platoons maneuvered against an NVA squad; they trapped the squad between them, but they were so close together that, when they shot into the NVA squad, they shot into each other. Each thought the other was the NVA and the two platoons had a brisk little firefight, until they called for artillery, and artillery fire control noticed that something was amiss. Several soldiers were wounded.

And then a private returned to us. He had fallen for the extension scam (re-up for six months on line and we'll send you home right now, fifteen days leave), but he had extended when we were near the peaceful little hamlet of Hoc Mon and he had returned to the anything-but-peaceful hamlet of Co Trach. While out on patrol near Ben Chua, he borrowed a .45, put the muzzle to his head, and pulled the trigger. (A grunt standing beside him said, "Ah, that son of a bitch! Now we have to carry him.")

Bad luck and good luck went hand in hand. Lt. Stinson was a lucky guy. He had gone through Jungle School and Division Orientation with me and then he had been assigned to "C" Company to replace Lt. Damron (who had been lightly wounded). Within the week he was sent out on a night ambush, two NVA entered his killzone, and he got them. Two days later a VC on a bicycle entered the killzone during a daytime ambush. And a few days after that, while he was returning from an ambush, he spotted a bunker complex.

"Okay, men," he said, "let's check it out."

He reorganized his platoon, so that he was third man behind the two men on point. Then he moved out. One of the point men suddenly noticed a pot of rice . . . steam rising into the air.

"Christ, sir, what are we getting into?"

An ambush.

The NVA threw grenades. Lt. Stinson was hit several times, once above the eye. Blood ran down his face. He ordered his men to pull the casualties out, while he remained behind, returned fire, and tossed grenades to cover them. When they were safe he crawled back to them and examined his injuries.

"What the hell, I can see. My nuts are still there. Let's go get them."

The medic grabbed him and the RTO called a dust-off. Lt. Stinson was sent to Japan and, from there, home. He had been in-country about a month. (Lt. Damron, whose place he had taken, was not so lucky. He returned to his platoon and was killed in an ambush.)

By now our operation had become a tourist attraction. Generals dropped out of the blue, posed for a few pictures with "the men," threw an arm around a lieutenant here and there, checked on the number of hearts and minds that had been won (or bodies that had been counted), and collected a citation.

The visits forced the troops to put on boots, cover bare skin and otherwise look strak, which was a bore, but the generals had a lot of fun and no harm was done, except, once in a while, to a general's ego, because the G.I.'s didn't respect generals; they respected the other guys on line— and no one else—and they didn't want to be bothered with lifer garbage, such as wearing a helmet on a hot day in the middle of the fire support base—on the ground within reach, while sitting, is close enough, or so, at least, one G.I. thought.

"Is that your helmet, soldier?" a visiting general demanded.

"Yeah," the soldier replied.

He was seated. He did not stand up.

"Yeah what?" barked one of the staff sycophants.

"Yeah, that's my helmet," the soldier said.

Who were these crazy dudes?

The general was no fool—he beat a retreat.

On 16 November I was at Fire Support Base Mahone. We had been there three weeks. We had knocked down hootches, cut back brush, and cleared fields of fire; we sent out patrols every day, we ambushed the area at night, we fired daily artillery missions at suspected enemy locations; in short, we vigorously prosecuted the war and still the war was one step past our wire.

A general was on hand that afternoon when a platoon patrol set out. The area they had to cross before they entered the boonies was now completely open except for one lone hootch right smack in the middle, and who would have thought anyone would hunker down in such an isolated hootch and shoot at an armed rifle platoon?

Bang!

The platoon hit the ground. Just like a training film, I thought. Team A laid down cover. Team B maneuvered left to flank the hootch. I could see tracers tearing through the grass walls. The walls smoked. Now Team B provided cover. Team A advanced and hit the ground, so Team B could advance, close enough to toss grenades. The grenades exploded and with a yell the platoon rushed forward. We heard a quick burst of firing. And silence.

The general was jumping up and down on the top of a bunker.

"They got him! They got him!"

His staff was composing the citation . . . cool direction under fire . . . disregarding his own safety . . .

A medic described it all later.

"That little bastard would've committed suicide just to take one of us with him."

"Mmmm," I said.

He held his hands an inch apart.

"He missed me that much."

"Well . . . ," I said.

"He was trying to hit me."

I nodded.

"Me!"

"Hey, don't take it personally."

The AO was rough. Lt. Cleveland's platoon was engaged in a firefight. He raised his head to look around and he was killed.

"He shouldn't have stuck his head up," someone said.

"Sometimes," Lt. Brown said, "when you're the leader, you've got to."

One of the Wolfhound lieutenants detailed to the 25th Division Infantry School (in Cu Chi) had lifted his head during the battle for Hoc Mon and a grenade fragment had pierced his throat. An APC officer brought his vehicle broadside in front of the lieutenant and pulled him to safety.

He agreed with Lt. Brown.

"Sometimes the lieutenant has to look."

We could not shake our hoodoo either. The Battalion surgeon (Captain Paul Shields) was ordered to investigate the case of a private who shot himself in the foot with his M-16.

"If he did it on purpose," the CO said, "I want him nailed."

The bullet had entered above the ankle. Every bone in the foot was powdered.

The surgeon told the CO, "The kid's going to lose his foot and part of the leg. A person would have to be crazy to shoot himself with an M-16."

The bullet destroys eight inches of bone at the point of impact. Then it tumbles. I once saw a bullet strike a standing man in the chest and exit at his knee.

A few days before, in a brief encounter with the NVA a grenadier fired his M-79, the grenade hit a tree, bounced back, and wounded two G.I.'s, not seriously, but still . . . another accident. That evening Colonel Reese delivered a lecture.

"Gentlemen, this reminds me of a story about Alexander the Great and the elephants. Alexander the Great knew he was going to meet some elephants in a battle and he figured out a way to turn them back on their own handlers and the elephants did turn back and trample their own troops, because, gentlemen, elephants cannot tell friend from foe. Now, does anyone see the point I am trying to make?"

"Yes sir," Lieutenant Brown said. "Never give a grenade launcher to an elephant."

Lt. Brown was an excellent S-5. He had trained the children to shout, "Woof'oun, woof'oun!" He put concrete collars around the local wells to prevent dirt from falling into the water. He was identifying, and targeting, the people in the hamlet.

I visited Co Trach with him. He and I and two security personnel handed out butter, milk, cigarettes, candy, and a pair of glasses. One woman lingered at the fringe of the crowd and wouldn't get in line for the food.

"Her husband is a VC," he said.

After the medcap we returned to Mahone and I waited for the convoy. The convoy was not being shot up as much, perhaps because a few days before B-52's had struck at the NVA base camp. One bomb makes a crater the size of a large living room, fifteen to twenty feet deep. The planes fly so high they might not even be visible, and anyone within a thousand meters of the bomb is killed. The strike had killed over 200 NVA.

Nonetheless, our convoy still attracted attention; miles away we could hear the confused sounds of small-arms fire.

"Hmm," a connoisseur said, "I detect a strong flavor of M-16 with a heavy accent of AK-47 and—Whoops!—heavy overtones of RPG with a dash of rocket and a lacing of M-60."

"Bake it for an hour in a napalm sauce and what do you have?"

"The Wolfhound convoy!"

"And the chef?"

"Magnet!"

A cloud of dust, screeching tires, a flood of invective—Magnet had arrived. He bounced from the jeep.

"Why me? Why is it always me?"

He shoved up his goggles.

"And the Mole . . . You know what the Mole says?"

The Mole—he wore thick glasses—was the driver.

"They practically blow us apart with an RPG. I feel the heat from it. Is my face scorched? Is my hair grey? It almost rips my blouse off. And you know what he says? He says, 'Gee, I don't like that sound.' "

"Well," the Mole said, "I don't like that sound."

"It's not enough, Mole. It's just not enough."

Every part of Magnet was in motion.

"Why me? Why not Captain Wong once in a while? Why me? What have I done?"

"I think this is just Charlie's way of saying he cares."

"And I've got to go back."

People gathered to enjoy the spectacle—Magnet Freaking Out—but I was going to ride the convoy and I didn't see the joke. I locked and loaded as we cleared the wire and passed the dead woman in the ditch; the NVA shot at us. We shot back. Gunships fired rockets into the brush. A jet dropped napalm. The noise was so great, I couldn't hear my own M-16 fire, and I never heard the bullets which struck the door and I didn't notice the holes until I was back in the motor pool and Lt. Artman met me and pointed them out.

"Mice?" he asked.

"Where was I when they were made?"

"Better not to know. Let's go get a beer."

Eventually, the enemy decided that the pleasure of shooting at the convoy wasn't worth the grief that followed. The napalm and the rockets, the artillery and the mortars, those were the least of it—worse for the enemy was the aggressive spirit of the Wolfhounds. Sergeant Mullens ("A" Company) was riding the convoy when he received fire. He and his men returned the fire and gained fire superiority. He wanted to strip the convoy of its personnel and go into the brush after the ambushers.

"I know I got one of them," he said. "I could feel blood."

The NVA might have thought of the road as their own. They kept it under observation. They stopped the Coke girls (who came down the road as soon as it was cleared), they collected some beer, lay in the weeds drinking a brew till afternoon when the Coke girls returned, they stopped them again, and collected a road tax in cash and kind. Occasionally they laid a mine. Every now and then they took a flier at a passing truck or at the squad strong points.

They might still have thought of the road as their own, but, in fact, the road now belonged to us.

PART IV

Visits to a Small Village

(20 November–27 December 1968)

Blacklist Blues

I got those blues, those blues, those blacklist blues.
  O don't you beat me, baby, with the old one-two.
  Don't break my ankle bones beneath your shoe.
  Don't stomp my bladder till the blood leaks through.
  Don't hurt me badder, baby—I'll be true . . .
Cuz I got those blacklist, black and blue list, blues.

Chapter 8

IT TAKES ALL KINDS

The first enlisted man I ever encountered at the 1/27th was a private in starched jungle fatigues who threw me a snappy salute and said,

"Sir, if you get a line company, will you take me with you? I'm sick of rear area duty."

"Sure," I said.

"Name's Private Young," he said. "Don't forget it, sir."

"Okay, Private Young."

What a strak young man. And how like a Wolfhound, I thought, just itching to get at the enemy. Later, as adjutant, I discovered that the itch seemed to be missing in many a Wolfhound. Every day my desk was covered with a pile of requests for transfer, transfer anywhere (except to another infantry unit). Transfer was a ticket to survival.

Disapproved.

"I want a job in the rear," a private said to me.

"Why?"

"I'm afraid out there, sir."

"How long have you been out there?"

"Six months."

"That's not so long."

"Sir, you just don't know."

"You're not the only one who's scared. What about the others out there?"

"That's their problem. I still want a transfer."

Disapproved.

Officers did not request a job off line, they requested a change of branch. Transportation was popular. So was Quartermaster. Intelligence was suspect—you might get lucky and do your tour in Saigon stoking the giant computer, but you might just as easily find yourself leading a three-man scout team into Laos.

I was supposed to forward these requests, but I wasn't sure it was in the best interests of the officers to do so. I thought they would have a different perspective after they came off line (promotion is faster in the Infantry—big turnover), and so . . .

Disapproved.

I was a good adjutant until I went to the field and learned compassion.

The adjutant was supposed to forward the junior officers' requests for their next duty station. If they stayed in, and survived the tour, they would rotate home for a year and then they would come back, and then, if they survived, they would go home for a year, and then come back, until they were killed, or the war ended, if the war ever did end.

"Well, Lt. Artman, what shall I put you down for?"

"THE WORLD!"

"Don't you like the Army?"

"Sure. Fun. Travel. Adventure."

"You meet interesting people."

"Tell me about it."

He hadn't found much common ground with his fellow recruits in Basic . . . or, for that matter, with his fellow officers.

"I was lying on my bunk one Saturday afternoon reading," he said. "Not being illiterate put me in the upper ten percentile—and one of the guys stopped.

" 'Geez, yuh sure read a lot, doncha?'

" 'Yes, I guess I do.'

" 'Yuh like tuh read, huh?'

" 'I would say that was a fair assumption.'

" 'I betcha redda hunnert books, aincha?'

" 'Yes, probably I have.'

" 'Whacha gonna do when yuh reddum all?'

"He thought there are maybe five hundred books in the world and at a hundred books a year, in four more years . . ."

So Lt. Artman intended to leave the Army, and I couldn't stamp . . . disapproved.

Then Private Young was marched to my desk by the medical service sergeant.

"Tenshut!"

Young crashed his heels together and delivered his textbook salute.

"Sir," the sergeant said, "I ordered Private Young to stay in the aid station area and he left."

"Is that right, private?"

"Permission to speak, sir!"

"Of course."

"Sir, there were some guys who needed help unloading a truck and I went and helped them."

"I found him at the EM club, sir."

"We went there after, sir. I forgot."

"Okay," I said. "That's not the issue. Did you understand the order you were given?"

"Yes sir!"

"Could you have asked the sergeant for permission to leave the area to unload that truck?"

"Yes sir!"

"Do you realize the seriousness of disobedience to orders?"

"Yes sir!"

"You could be court-martialled."

"Yes sir!"

"Well, then, it's up to the sergeant. What do you want to do, sergeant?"

"I want him to shape up."

"Okay. Private Young, you heard him. Is that possible? Are you going to attend to orders in the future?"

"Yes sir!"

"You won't get a second chance."

"Yes sir!"

"Dismissed."

He saluted, faced about, and marched out . . . hut . . . two . . . three . . . four. The sergeant shook his head. I waved him to a chair.

"What's going on, sergeant?"

"I think he's crazy."

"Crazy?"

"He just don't act normal. He says what a hero he is and how he's never afraid and then he hides so he don't have to go out and one time he rubs dog's blood in his eyes. And, like with the puppies, there was an order that we had too many mascots and the MPs came around and he led them over to another area where there were some puppies and he strangled them. I talked to the doc and I'd like to send him to see a psychiatrist."

I asked for a second opinion. Magnet knew Private Young.

"That crazo. I captured a gook pistol and I needed some nine mike-mike ammo so I went to supply. He was in supply then. He takes a look, works the slide like a pro, and says he carried a nine mike-mike himself when he walked up Highway One alone. He digs some ammo out.

Alone? I say. Nothing happened, he says. Alone? What a strak soldier, I think. Then he says, hey, sir, I want to get out in the field. What're the chances of getting in your platoon? Great! After he comes to my platoon, he writes his Congressman that he's tired of my always ordering him to kill women and children. We must have had two dozen goddamned reporters down here and some brassass from the IG."

When Young was out in the field, he killed and cut up a dog and rubbed its blood in his eyes, so he wouldn't have to go out on patrol. The platoon forced Young to go out anyway and then they trashed him.

The doc gave Young some medication, but Young took one or two pills and threw the rest away. ("He could feel his personality changing.") I sent him to a psychiatrist. The psychiatrist sent back a written report (and Young). I read it and then I phoned him.

"Doctor, there's no recommendation in your report."

"Well, we're encouraged not to give one."

"I understand."

Let the shrinks certify nut cases off line, goodbye Army.

"But I remember him quite well. He definitely has an unstable personality."

"Yeah, he's nuts—we already knew that—but is he fit for combat?"

"Well, you have to ask the question, is anyone really fit for combat? There you have a hyperstressed environment in which any abnormality, otherwise successfully compensated, could become disabling and, as it were, a psychosis, which, considered with the frenetic personality profile and the unstable tendencies, I would certainly have to give my opinion that it would be preferable that you not assign him to a front line unit."

"Doctor, we are a front line unit."

"Well . . ."

"Doctor, we want to get him off line. We can't do that unless we have a written recommendation from you."

I did the paper work for troops coming and going (alive and dead). I sent them home, one way or another, and I greeted them.

"Men, welcome to the First Wolfhounds, the best Infantry unit in Vietnam . . . and hence the world."

I was not supposed to conceal the dangers.

"Some men sew a dogtag into their boot so what's left of the body can be identified. Now, you may be saying, if I get it, who cares whether they identify me or not? And I recognize that the uncertainty your relatives would face is not likely to weigh heavily on your minds . . ."

"You said it!" an anonymous voice popped off.

". . . but . . . ," I asked a soldier, ". . . what's your blood type?"

"I dunno, sir."

"Suppose you're wounded, you're lying on the operating table, you need an immediate transfusion, and you've lost your dogtags and they have to waste time typing you. Maybe you don't have time."

Then I explained about rockets.

"If you hear a funny whistling noise and everyone around you starts running, run after them."

(My successor, Lt. Brown, was delivering this lecture when he did hear a rocket. He dashed for the bunker. As he turned the corner, he glanced back. The troops were huddled together like a flock of sheep. "Run!" he yelled.)

I finished my spiel and asked for questions.

A private raised his hand.

"Sir, is it true that the Wolfhounds used dum-dum bullets in Korea?"

Chapter 9

S-5

True to the Battalion's new spirit of aggressiveness, Colonel Reese chased a VC with his loach. On the twenty-fourth of November he was making a recon in his loach, he saw a VC on the ground, and he pursued; he fired off two magazines with his CAR-15, threw several frag grenades, and reported "one possible body count."

On the same day back in Mahone Lt. Maurer was wounded by mortar fire. Lt. Maurer had always had a smile on his face, had smiled even in the bad days of the summer of '68, even when he left the wire in pursuit of the bad guys. He might even smile during a firefight. That was the problem.

"Gee, look at that!"

"What!"

"Those clouds. They look just like a . . ."

"Uh, sir, shouldn't we call some artillery?"

"Hey, yeah, good idea. Let's do that."

The first round that hit Mahone destroyed the counter-mortar radar set. Lt. Maurer looked around to make sure everyone had gotten into the bunkers and then he decided he had better seek shelter himself. He was entering the bunker when a round hit and blew him the rest of the way in. He tumbled against the opposite wall and, as he lay there, he wondered, "Why am I lying here against the wall . . . ?" until he heard a sergeant say, "Hell, they got Lt. Maurer."

I visited him at the hospital. He looked grey and misshapen from shock and loss of blood. His condition improved, however, when he learned that he was going to be sent to Japan.

My morale improved, too. At the end of November I was transferred to the job of S-5. The S-5 team then consisted of two medics (Leonard and Lopez), an Arvn interpreter (Tien), and Private Robert Kirksey.

Private Kirksey was nursing a grudge. When he took the Selective Service examination, he was told that those who flunked would not be eligible for the draft (no matter how much they whined and begged), so he flunked. Lots of examinees flunked. You might say the only ones who passed were those too dumb to flunk. Subsequently, however, the selective service lowered the passing grade and retested the flunkers, one of whom was Kirksey.

"Listen up, men," a sergeant announced. "Forget that last exam you took. It don't mean squat. This is the only exam that counts and there ain't no way to flunk it, cuz you've already passed, just by being here, so do your best, cuz the better you do, the better job you'll get."

Kirksey did do his best, he scored the highest in his group . . . and he was assigned to the Infantry. He thought he had a grievance and he went on strike.

All officers and men in the Brigade had to attend a five-day orientation course before going to the field. The five-day course was supposed to give the newcomers a chance to pick up a few tips, acclimatize, and generally settle down. Kirksey refused to go; if he had to attend the course before he went to the field, he wouldn't attend the course and then he wouldn't have to go to the field. He had evaded the course for two months, though part of that period had been spent in the LBJ lock up, which time is the baddest time there is—it doesn't come off the tour.

Major Lynch (the XO) had him come into the office. (Colonel Reese had suggested that Major Lynch have the largest soldier in the Battalion standing by when he gave Kirksey the news that he had to go, but the major replied, "He is the largest soldier in the Battalion.")

When Major Lynch told him, Kirksey yelled, "I won't go!"

He slammed his fists down on the desk in front of the XO.

"I won't go . . . sir."

"Now you're acting like a baby," Major Lynch said. "You're going to go."

The major took him by the arm, said, "Come on now," and led him to school.

The major then told me, "Get him through Orientation. I don't care how you do it."

I, from the varied and fruitful experience of graduate school politics and a year in the army, said this, "Private, you can't fight City Hall."

And I was City Hall.

I went to the sergeant who took attendance for Orientation and I asked him to mark Kirksey present at all sessions. Roger, sir, and Kirksey officially completed Orientation.

After he "graduated," he still managed to avoid going to the field. He demanded compassionate leave so he could go home and kill the S-O-B who was messing around with his wife.

"Look! I got pictures!"

The pictures seemed less than compelling to me, but I approved the request. Leave . . . and God go with you. Within the hour the Brigade Adjutant called.

"Come on now, Captain. I know what you're trying to do, and I sympathize, but this just doesn't cut it."

So Kirksey demanded to see the Inspector General (IG), as was his right, and I made an appointment for him (and wished him well). The IG did not grant the request for compassionate leave, but he had arranged an appointment with a team of three medical specialists, the specialists had examined Kirksey, tut-tutted at the skin rash under his chin, and they had given him a profile, that is, a restriction on his activity: He was not to be compelled to shave or to participate in any activity which might cause him to perspire, though he could, if he wished, volunteer to go out to the field, hump a pack and rifle, and let it all hang out. Kirksey played a lot of basketball.

And then, suddenly one morning, he showed up at the motor pool, said, "I'm tired of the rear area," got on a truck, and went out to Mahone. He was assigned to the S-5 (me) and, I must say, he really put his heart and soul into the hearts and minds game.

Later I was assigned the Permanent Private. In his nineteen years of service the Permanent Private had been up and down the promotion ladder several times; he had been sergeant (E-5), he had been staff sergeant (E-6), and once he had even made first sergeant (E-7), only to tumble off the ladder again. Whiskey was his ruin . . . and grass.

My primary mission was to win hearts and minds. My secondary mission, given to me by Colonel Reese, was to stamp out the world's oldest profession. Prostitutes had set up shop at the edge of the fire support base and there they waited for their customers. Sometimes—their intelligence was excellent—we would lift into some outlying hamlet, storm into the LZ with artillery and rockets, tumble out, form a perimeter, and see the prostitutes waving at us. They were welcome everywhere there were soldiers, G.I. or NVA.

If we had ever gotten their cooperation, we could have nailed every VC and NVA in our Area of Operation. We did receive snippets of information (one of which probably saved my life), but so did the NVA.

The girls had a living to make, and spilling what they knew would have cost them their living, if not their lives.

So I was prostitute control officer. Free penicillin (for the girls, I mean). Free counseling. Have you ever considered a career as a tour guide or perhaps a stenographer? Regular checkups.

The prostitutes—what did you do in the last war, daddy? Well, darling, I was prostitute control officer—knew my assignment and they tried to work their wiles on me.

"Souvenir one time?" Madam Fred asked.

"No, thank you."

"What madder you—you no like girls?"

"I'm just afraid you wouldn't respect me afterwards."

"Wha'?"

The prostitutes were small-town girls who wanted to travel, see some of the world, and have some fun; they never ceased to be amazed that they could be their own source of income. At first, they were so naive that they didn't demand cash in advance and believed the soldiers who refused to pay because "it wasn't any good." Then a large Cambodian woman (we called her Madam Fred) took over and organized them— woe now to the grunt who maltreated a girl; no skin for the duration.

I was ordered to stamp out prostitution, not for moral reasons, but because, while Madam Fred was a good sport, and she was useful, neither she nor her girls had seen the same training films we had. The medics were kept busy.

"These guys," Lt. Artman said. "They don't do anything to take care of themselves. They're not going to see thirty."

"Maybe they think they should enjoy it while they can."

"And some of the officers . . ."

Lt. Artman thought officers should be gentlemen.

". . . wives at home and living here with a native woman."

"Shades of W. Somerset Maugham."

"I certainly didn't rush into marriage myself. My friends didn't believe I'd ever get married. They didn't believe it when we sent out the invitations. They still didn't believe it the day of the wedding. My best man had already figured out what he would say to the bride. Even she thought I might not show up."

Meanwhile, the . . . uh . . . problem came to the notice of the chaplain. (He wasn't concerned about officers and their hootch-maids because he didn't believe that an officer, and a married man to boot, would consort with a native woman. I mean, why would he?) But he was incensed about the prostitutes. He demanded that the CO order the men to cease consorting with the brazen jezebels and harlots.

"What about their sweethearts at home? What about their mothers? Isn't it bad enough that they might lose their lives?"

Sorry, boy (says the Lord), you have known the whore of Babylon, you have revelled in the fleshpots of Sodom and Co Trach, you have grovelled in the dung of Dau Tieng. You are going to have to go Down There.

"Well, Padre, I'll see what I can do."

"If you don't stop them, Colonel, I shall have to speak to Brigade."

The CO, after his jaws unclamped, asked the doctor to give the men a talk.

"Men," Dr. Shields began, "you've all heard about that little island off Japan."

Some grunts from World War II are still in quarantine because they caught The Big Crud. Three days after you catch it, your dick turns green . . . and then it falls off. You become a walking pus-bag. Pus drips from your ears, eyes, and nose. So dangerous was this strain of VD that a decision was made at the highest levels—"What if Eleanor should catch it?"—to quarantine the afflicted on a little island off Japan. Later, G.I.'s from Korea were sent there, and if YOU'RE not careful . . .

"Men, you've got a raw deal here," our doctor said, "and if the only way you can have fun is consorting with those whores, go to it. I can cure anything you can catch."

"Doctor," the CO said, "that is not what I had in mind."

And so the girls, and the hamlet, were put off limits, but they were still there, and where they were was where I went every day to conduct a medcap. I was extremely popular.

The G.I.'s who went along with me, either on my team or as security (we took security into the village because some of the natives resented our desire to win their hearts and minds), could look forward to the pleasures of the village: Fifty cents for a beer, fifteen dollars for a prostitute, one time only, in the bush, the village children watching.

Kirksey was popular with all the "girls" and especially popular with one we called Slash. Slash (a nickname given her not because of her profession but because of her face—the burn tissue, the long thick scar, the missing eyeball) fell in love with Kirksey.

"I love you too much . . ."

She touched her belly.

". . . I sick here."

"Hey, baby," he said, "that's the way to talk."

Chapter 10

CHIEU HOI

Chieu hoi means "to come over." The one who comes over is a hoi chanh. Hoi chanhs expressed many reasons for coming over.

"I VC ten month—all time B-52 drop bomb—number 10—now I chieu hoi—B-52 number one!"

A would-be hoi chanh came up to the wire one night and called out, "Chieu hoi!"

When no one responded, he laid down his rifle and walked through the wire into the fire support base. He wandered from bunker to bunker but couldn't find anyone awake. Finally, he went up to the 4.2-inch mortar platoon, which was firing their nightly H&I. He tugged at the sleeve of one of the mortarmen and said, "Chieu hoi!"

"Beat it!" the soldier said. (He thought the defector was a Kit Carson scout.)

The VC went back outside the wire, sat down, and tried to figure out what to do. He decided to walk around the perimeter one more time, yelling, "Chieu hoi!" and finally a G.I. from "A" Company heard him.

The final straw in his career as VC, he said, was when a woman was appointed commander . . . and she refused to give him a hammock.

The hoi chanh fingered eleven VC—the wife of the VC village chief, the cook for the local VC, and nine other members of the VC infrastructure—and he reported that the VC had discussed ways and means of terminating the daily medcaps.

One of the medics I liked to take with me when he was available was Spec-4 Touchberry. I liked his sense of humor, his compassion, and his toughness.

"I'm thinking of getting married," he said one day.

"Yeah?"

"Yes sir. Who do I have to ask for permission to marry?"

"It depends. Who's the lucky girl?"

"Madam Fred."

"See the chaplain."

"Will the army transfer me away from her?"

"Sure," I said. "Ever hear of the Marine Corps?"

He took me to an isolated grass hootch occupied by an old man—old enough to me, anyway—who had books, mostly yellow-spined French paperbacks, but also an English dictionary.

"Hello," the old man said.

"Hello."

"How are you?"

"Fine."

"Welcome to my home."

"Thank you."

"Do you want beaver eggs?"

"What?"

"Beaver eggs?"

His finger traced the letters in the palm of his hand: B E V E R A G E S. I pronounced it for him. He repeated the word carefully.

"Beverages. Do you want beverages?"

We had been warned about fraternizing—hepatitis, TB, amoebic dysentery, the creeping crud—but a civic action officer can't turn down proffered hospitality, and, anyway, hepatitis, TB, and The Big Squirt were all tickets out of the field.

"Tea?" he suggested.

"All right. Thank you."

We had tea and honey.

"He's teaching me Vietnamese," Touchberry said.

"Ah," I said.

"Good student," the old man said.

"Where did you learn English?" I asked.

"I teach myself," he said.

"And French?"

"I was sergeant d'infanterie. How do you say?"

"Infantry sergeant."

"Oui. Parlez-vous français?"

"Ne qu'un peu."

"Un peu?"

He shook his head with disappointment at the young barbarian. The gooks kicked out the frogs, lock, stock, and barrel, but they can't kick their culture. We drank the tea, Touchberry handed over a can of

C-rations and a package of chewing tobacco, the old man thanked us, and we left.

"He's something else, isn't he, sir?"

"Yes," I said. "Probably VC."

Nonetheless I preferred him to the committed anti-communist I soon met.

"There's some gook here to see you," Lopez said.

"Where?" I asked, and into my palace—a 3/4-ton truck with a canopy spread for shade beside a two-person bunker—sauntered an Arvn, a vision of loveliness from his head (red beret with badge) down to his spit-shined, jungle-booted tootsies.

("Dig the skin-tight tiger fatigues," Leonard whispered.)

He carried a polished swagger stick with a glistening metal tip and he had a black list. (A black list is a list of suspects compiled from information provided by people who are supposed to know.)

"Well, chung-wi," I said, "and what can we do for you?"

He pulled out a cigarette, lit it, and flourished it in the three-finger reverse hold of the Hollywood gestapo agent.

He was Lt. Nhut, leader of an Arvn Psyops team. Psyops go out, walk around the village, talk to the people, and collect information. Lt. Nhut was not bad, as Arvn spooks go. He discovered the location of a mortar platoon and a VC squad. He learned about the local problems—a child orphaned by mortar fire, people whose rice crop had been destroyed by our landing pad—and he also uncovered a tunnel, a tunnel which began in the middle of the hamlet and ended at an outlying hut, a hut which just happened to have been incorporated by us into the fortifications of Mahone, five meters from the S-5 palace.

Oops.

We turned a flamethrower loose on it.

Villagers were coming forward to give us information and to ask us for help and I began to have ideas. Perhaps we could set up a school in the hamlet and have the old man teach the children. I was not sure where his loyalties lay, but he was intelligent and educated, and he was more patriotic than most Vietnamese, who have little idea of their own history. I did have doubts about the soundness of introducing the village children to the great wide world out there, only to have them discover, as inevitably they must, that that world was closed to them because they weren't from the "right" family.

I discussed the project with the old man. He was willing, but after serving me tea and honey the old man told me a story. At the time, perhaps, I didn't get the point.

"Long ago the Chinese . . ."

He scowled as he spoke the word.

". . . the Chinese invade Vietnam. They demand we give them land. They say, *you fight our Chinese bull with Vietnamese bull. Our bull win, we take Vietnam.* We have no great bull, but we say okay. We take young baby—how you say?"

"Calf."

"We take caff from mother. It cry. It want mother. We keep one . . . two . . . three day. Chinese come. Have bull. We give caff. Bull attack. Caff think bull be mother. Try drink. Bull try get away. Caff try drink. Bull run. We keep our Vietnam."

Vietnamese myths demonstrate cleverness and cunning, not self-sacrifice. The children needed instruction. They certainly needed discipline. Whenever we entered the village, the children swarmed around us, begging for candy and toys and clothes.

"Woof'ouns! Woof'ouns!"

"OK, G.I."

"You got M-16."

"You got one two three four five M-26 frag grenade."

I gave a blouse to a cute little girl. Her neighbor punched her in the nose and grabbed the blouse. The little girl cried.

"Sorry 'bout that."

The other little girl hit her again. The first girl's brother punched the second little girl. The second little girl's brother punched the first little girl's brother. A free-for-all began. The blouse was shredded.

Kids, I might say, do your parents scramble and brawl and turn into complete idiots when we distribute rice?

Yes.

Right! Nevertheless, no line, no chop-choppie.

The children believed that we had dropped from the skies to distribute candy and clothes and to play games with them; the adults were more suspicious. I was supposed to convince them that we were philanthropists, whose only goal was to make them happy: And if you think you've gotten good stuff now, just wait until the war has been won for Saigon. We could play the we-want-nothing game, because the NVA had to live off the land and we didn't. My spokesman was a Vietnamese named Son.

"Tell them, Son, that we have not come for their rice."

Son was a hoi chanh.

"Tell them we have not come to collect taxes."

A VC who had seen the light.

"Tell them we want nothing from them."

Son was also a tough dude.

"Tell them we have come to protect them."

In his mouth my gentle admonitions sounded like threats and our audience appeared unconvinced, if not downright puzzled and confused, so I hauled Son off to Sergeant Dai, the Arvn interpreter, for a conference.

"Tell him what you said, Son."

Son told him. Dai laughed. Son's ancestors had come to Vietnam from China a thousand years before; like many of the ethnic Chinese in Vietnam he spoke no Vietnamese.

The hoi chanhs who worked for us were called Kit Carson Scouts. We treated them like scout dogs: We fed them special rations and assigned each a handler. Touchberry brought one of them around to show to me.

"Meet Mighty Mouse, our trained monkey. He doesn't know what monkey means, but he knows what he has to know."

Mighty Mouse was a very small Vietnamese with a large rifle.

"Hi, Mouse," I said.

"Hi, Daiwi."

"Chico," Touchberry said, "decided to blow up a bunker we found. He set the charge and yelled fire in the hole, and everyone passed it on. Fire in the hole! Fire in the hole!"

Mighty Mouse grinned.

"Fi-lah-ho!" he said.

"See. He speaks English."

By the middle of December the countryside had quieted down considerably—the convoy hadn't been shot at in over two weeks, the mechanized infantry only occasionally hit a mine, and the villagers came out and waved at us. Magnet rotated away and his place was taken by an officer from the Transportation Corps.

This officer, Lt. Handley, was not ecstatic at being in an Infantry battalion, or at running the convoys, but he soon learned to put up a good front and with a flash of teeth and a salute would say, "Can do, sir!"

Major Cox (our new XO) tried to convince him to transfer to the Infantry.

"Where's your spirit of adventure, Handley?"

"I don't have any, sir. I'm a coward."

"Do you want to go through your tour hiding in a nice safe job while others go out exposing themselves to danger?"

"Yes sir, I do."

Running the convoy was not a safe occupation. A driver from Supply and Transportation (not 1/27th Infantry) drove over to our motor pool and Lt. Handley asked him, "Do you have your flak jacket?"

"No sir."

"Do you have a weapon?"

"No sir."

"Do you have a steel pot?"

"No sir."

"Well, you'd better get them. You may be going on the convoy."

"The Wolfhound convoy?" he asked in awe.

"Right. Or more probably you'll be making track runs around the Ammo Supply Point."

"The Wolfhound Ammo Supply Point?"

Lt. Handley had just become inured to the regular convoy run, when (in the middle of December, to beat the Christmas truce) Brigade decided that the Wolfhounds should establish a fort in the Michelin not far from a Ruff-Puff fort. Brigade also decided that the fort would be supplied by road.

"I'm glad I don't have to do it," Major Cox said to Lt. Handley, "but that's why we have centurions . . . to take the risks and get killed."

The NVA mined the roads and attacked the fort. They were driven back and the convoys went through. By the end of December the fort was well established.

The dry season had arrived with a vengeance. The grass turned brown and the dogs (native mongrel and army scout) took to sleeping through the day and padding about in the night. Fires, started mostly through human agency, burned continuously and a pall of smoke hung over our AO.

For two months, now, we had been operating in an area the NVA considered vital. The NVA had sworn that Americans would never penetrate that area. We had. The NVA had predicted that we would be driven out. We hadn't been. The NVA tried to prevent our using the roads. They couldn't.

By the end of December I no longer needed security to enter the hamlet of Co Trach. The interpreters walked freely through the whole of the hamlet and sometimes spent the night. The children, and many of the adults, associated with us and talked openly about the VC—who they were, where they were, and when they could be expected to return. Six VC gave up before Christmas.

Colonel Reese commanded the First Wolfhounds in the beginning phase of the pacification of Tri Tam district, one of the most successful operations of the war. He rekindled the Wolfhound spirit, but—soldiers are superstitious—he could not shake the Wolfhound jinx. Its last victim, late in December, was Colonel Reese himself. As he boarded his loach for a recon, his knee struck the joystick, the loach lurched and it pitched him out. He broke both wrists and had to be evacuated to Japan. He was the last victim of the Wolfhound jinx.

His replacement was LTC James Meredith.

PART V

The Flying S-5

(28–29 December 1968)

The Evening News

"This week we've learned that ten G.I.'s were greased."
(With sepulchral tones old smoothie reads the news.)
"But on a sadder note . . . also deceased
Was CBS reporter Robert Trewes."

"He was a correspondent once for *Life*—
Before he worked for us. We all miss Bob
And send regrets to Ann, his grieving wife."
(The ten G.I.'s? Too bad, but that's their job.)

Chapter 11

LITTLE DID I KNOW

We received orders to make a show of force in the Michelin plantation, to go where no one (Occidental) had gone before (except the French Foreign Legion) and to hoist the yellow flag (with three red stripes). The NVA had said that we were afraid to go, but if we came anyway, they would annihilate us.

I was ordered to go along—to carry the flag—and I was excited and nervous about my first combat mission, the chance of contact, and my first helicopter ride (except for one with seat belts and closed doors in the Canal Zone).

On 28 December 1968, just after dawn, I stood on the PZ and waited for the helicopters. All around me were small groups of restless, voiceless men . . . yawning, coughing, shuffling their feet, adjusting the straps of their webbing gear, checking their equipment, counting their grenades. And then, far off, I heard a stuttering noise beating toward me, specks above the horizon, slicks rushing at me, dead weight slung beneath a rotor looking like bumblebees in a panic, darting to the PZ.

They touched, we sprinted forward, clambered on board, me first, so I could grab the middle seat and not be next to the open door. I glanced at the door gunner, bloodshot eyes, shaky hands, clenched teeth, and I glanced at the pilots. The pilots liked to say that they were even crazier than the Infantry, and we had to agree with them. A friend of mine back at Benning had asked a pilot (up in the air) about autorotation.

"Does the main rotor blade really act like a parachute?"

"Sure," the pilot said . . . and shut off the engine to demonstrate.

In a normal tour a pilot could expect to crash ten times; they think crashing is just another way of landing.

The giant rotor yanked us into the air. I tried to speak and couldn't hear my own voice over the throbbing of the blade. The chopper lurched and I slid across the seat . . . toward an open door . . . and men were sitting beside the open doors? What if the slick did a lateral ninety? But no one appeared worried, at least about being dumped, and no one had fastened a seat belt, so I couldn't fasten mine, not and appear cool.

My first flight—in a bouncing helicopter, among armed men, rushing through a sky filled with falling artillery and machine gun fire . . . Suddenly the LZ appeared, coming at us, fast. We're going to crash, I thought, but no, we touched down and everything was normal in a perfectly routine flight.

I tumbled off, fell flat, and wriggled for a low spot. Were we taking fire? I listened. I couldn't hear anything that sounded like in-coming, but what did I know? I raised my head and looked around for someone, anyone, and saw . . . nobody. Shouldn't somebody be giving directions? Where was the village? Where is everyone?

A whistle blew. Men rose all around me, like lumps of clay on resurrection day. Captain Charles Ervin and the command group of Charlie Company were clearly marked by the forest of radio antennas and I, the true neophyte, joined them and walked with them toward the village, which (I now could see) lay half-concealed in the tangled foliage at the edge of the LZ. As we drew nearer, I could distinguish huts, regularly spaced and separated by beaten paths, but I didn't see any people and I was about to ask where they were when I heard sharp cracks in the air and the captain and his command group went to the ground.

Cracks in the air? I thought. Everyone around me going flat? This must be in-coming!

I picked a soft patch of ground, no rocks, mud, or miscellaneous debris, and I settled in beside Ervin and the others and with them crawled up behind the plastered wall of a hootch, where we felt safe . . . until the RTO pushed his fist through it.

"Oops," he said.

"Hell, that wall won't stop . . ."

Holes the size of cantaloupes appeared above our heads.

Whomp . . . whomp . . . whomp . . .

A machine gun with a slow cycle of fire, as though someone were shooting it off with a crank. A .51 caliber.

"I don't like the looks of this," Captain Ervin said. He was a master of understatement.

I didn't like it either and I tried to make sense of the medley of small arms fire: What were we facing? Who was winning? How worried should I be?

Captain Ervin got on the horn.

"Three, this is One, over."

"One, Three, over."

"What do you have? Over."

"A couple AKs, .51, squad maybe. Over."

"Do you need support? Over."

"Negative. Over."

The calm voice of the platoon leader reassured me, I relaxed a little, and my training reasserted itself, so that I could separate friendly noise from enemy noise, and tell that the U.S. noise—grenades, M-60s, and rifles—had grown in volume while the NVA noise had diminished; we were winning . . . if that was a consolation when a single slug from a .51 can tear your leg off. I searched the ground for a spot where I could scratch a hole.

"Any whiskeys? Over."

A LAW exploded. The .51 stopped firing. Had we nailed it?

"Negative. I think Victor has di-died."

Got clean away.

No bodies. No blood trails. They drifted off like ghosts, and we had to ask, where had they gone? Through a tunnel into the village? Would they now pose as innocent villagers? Would they ambush us from the huts? Would they reappear outside the village?

A squad collected the inhabitants and we asked them these questions —how many NVA are there, where are they, will they return—and we learned that the NVA main force, which hoped very much to meet some Americans, had departed, not three hours before, for the village where their intelligence had predicted we would land first. The villagers expected the main force to return, soon, and they were tense, and so were we.

"Okay, S-5," Captain Ervin said, "let's not just stand around. Do your stuff."

Right. I ran up the flag, delivered a speech (Our Friend the Saigon Government), and I held a medcap.

An old woman, the village midwife as it turned out, tugged at my sleeve.

"This woman," my interpreter said, "she say . . . uh . . . woman have baby. Much pain. Much trouble. You help?"

I asked Leonard and Lopez, my two medics, if they were willing; they were. She led them through the village to an isolated hut, where the prospective mother, hardly more than a child herself, writhed in pain. The midwife spoke to her: I've brought two American doctors trained in the finest medical schools of the West and now everything will be okay.

Then she settled back, chewed her betel nut, and spit.

Lopez took over.

"Don't get your womb in a whirl, mama-san," he said. "Leonard and Lopez are here."

Labor had already begun.

"You work the top, Leonard, and I'll catch the kid."

He laid out his equipment.

"Keep it up, mama, I can feel the baby coming."

All was going well and then . . .

An RPG exploded. The woman screamed.

What ran through my mind, Lopez said, *was one, we've had it; two, contract like hell, mama; and, three, what a world for a kid to come into.*

AKs. AKs always sound like they're going off in your ear. The mother lost her concentration. Leonard wiped her forehead.

"No sweat, mama-san, no sweat."

Leonard seemed so calm, Lopez said, *it was only later that it occurred to me that he had become a soprano.*

The midwife spoke sharply to the woman: Stop this nonsense! The woman moaned, but she obeyed, and the baby's head emerged.

I grabbed that little bugger and yanked him out and tied him off before you could say natural birth.

"Give her a dose of penicillin, Leonard, and let's di-di."

Then, Lopez said, *I looked around and there was this man.*

A man? He wasn't armed, but he was of an age to be armed. He spoke to the midwife and pointed at the medics and she spoke and pointed at the mother and then he beckoned to them.

I clutched. Should we follow him?

Who was he?

He patted me on the arm and said, "Number one."

The man led them through some hootches, around a large water jar, and to the edge of the square. There we were.

When the RPG went off, the villagers screamed and fled. I flopped and low-crawled into the school house; three men in strange uniforms leaped at me through the window. Half a second to react. By the time my hands worked the safety and my brain said shoot, I realized they were Americans in tiger suits. If they had been NVA, I would have been three times dead.

BAM!

Fragments slammed into the wall. We tried to go through the floor. Our own artillery, right on target. The NVA didn't wait for the rest of it; they had disrupted our visit, that was enough, and they vanished. We decided that we, too, had done what we came to do; we got together and started off.

I have to reconstruct what happened next, since it happened below the level of my conscious mind, but as I walked back through the village, I must, without realizing it, have been picking out points of cover, because, first, I heard a vicious ripping noise, and, second, I found myself lying behind a large rock on the other side of a five-foot-high spiked fence, while in my mind I was seeing a kind of slow-motion replay of me vaulting over the spikes, and I was thinking, was that an AK?

My medics, too, had gone to cover, but at a more sedate pace.

"Take it easy, sir. That's just a slick."

Chapter 12

I LIE IN A PIGPEN

We broke into lifts on the PZ and scanned the sky. Come on, slicks, get us out of here.

Empty sky.

Where are they?

Here they come.

They touched down. We sprinted to them, scrambled in, I sprawled on the floor, and—yank—we were airborne so fast I didn't have a chance to get my balance. I slid a little toward the open door and Lopez grabbed my webbing.

"Long way down, sir."

But who could sweat the small stuff? Another village was coming. What would we find there? AKs? RPGs? Another .51? The NVA main force?

The door gunner touched my shoulder.

"LZ's hot."

How hot is hot, I wanted to ask, but he hunkered down behind his machine gun and pressed the trigger; cartridge cases flew through the air. One went down my neck . . . damn! . . . it burned. I wriggled. Lopez yelled, "I don't like this," and then we hit and he jumped out firing. Hunched over, I followed him, ran half-a-dozen steps, and went to cover, but no matter how I strained my ears, I couldn't hear the pops and whines and cracks that mean an LZ's hot. Had the door gunner exaggerated?

He had. Captain Ervin was already on his feet; I joined him and waited for the village to be secured. This village contained perhaps three dozen huts; the rifle company (it was larger on paper) had ninety or so men on the ground. Three dozen huts, ninety men, I didn't like the arithmetic—

whoever had to enter the village to collect the people would be hanging in the breeze—but Captain Ervin had to go with what he had and it wasn't my problem and, anyway, Captain Ervin seemed unperturbed.

"How you enjoying it so far?" he asked.

"Mere words can't do my feelings justice," I said.

He laughed. Then his RTO announced, "Security's in place."

"OK," Captain Ervin said to me. "You can go round up your people."

My people? Me? I did not want to go into that village, but I could see Captain Ervin's point of view—why risk his own men?—and I couldn't see that I had a choice, so I broke the news to my medics and to Sunny (Sergeant Tien, the Arvn interpreter)—they looked at me as though I were crazy—and I gritted my teeth, checked that the safety of my M-16 was off, and we entered the village. The people peeked at us from inside their huts. They were terrified.

"This is kinda scary," Leonard said.

Sunny yelled at them.

Gather at the school!

The people disappeared into their bunkers. He shouted some more.

No way, G.I.

We were almost through the village when Leonard whispered to me, "I'm puckered to a pinhead," and I decided enough was enough.

I paused for thought beside a shallow ditch.

CRACK!

I was lying in the shallow ditch. I felt a pain in my side.

I'm hit! I looked. Always look.

I was lying on a sharp rock.

AKs and M-16s were trading fire, but the AKs were on the other side of the M-16s (so far) and we were relatively okay, though none of us had any inclination to leave the ditch.

I heard the platoon leader, Lt. Roe, shout, "There! Put one there!"

A grenade went off. A machine gun fired. Another grenade went off. "I think it's time to leave," I said and my little group agreed with me . . . and so did the villagers. The villagers abandoned their huts and ran for the schoolhouse. The school was a substantial building with a concrete terrace and good, solid-looking walls, inside of which the whole village crouched and screamed. I stood close to a wall and listened to the firefight.

It didn't last long. We gained fire superiority, the NVA knocked off, and we sent out the word that we could go ahead with our program. The biggies landed—the Battalion CO, the Sergeant Major, and the District Chief of Tri Tam District. (An Arvn major and a conscientious guy, he was killed in an ambush on the road a year after we left.) The District Chief coaxed the people from the school and addressed them.

"My children, the RVN government is your government and I am here to serve you. The communists . . ."

An AK fired so close I could hear the bolt slide back and forth. I went flat. The people screamed and stampeded back into the schoolhouse. Ricocheting bullets and chips of concrete were flying all around. The Arvn Major tried to calm the people down. They kept screaming. Another AK fired. We were caught in the middle. There was no place to hide. This is it, I thought, when the Battalion CO yelled, "There they are!"

He raised his commando rifle and jerked the trigger. The rifle jammed just as Captain Ervin knocked the muzzle up.

"Those are ours!"

"Oh," the colonel said.

Panic.

Heck, I thought, now is not the time to lose your head. I'm not hit yet and there're lots bigger targets than me for the VC to snipe at. I low-crawled to the wall of the school and reconnoitered. The enemy was inside the perimeter, but apparently they were VC and they hesitated to fire into their friends and neighbors. Okay, then. I ducked into the school; the people did not exactly welcome me (like maybe they weren't so sure that the VC wouldn't fire into friends and neighbors) and I felt far from secure. I looked around for another hole and noticed a three-walled pigpen out the back; the company command group was already in it. I took off.

Pop! Pop! Pop!

I dove.

"Mother!"

My medics had found the pigs' bunker next to the pigpen. Sunny was inside the schoolhouse. The biggies followed me, crowded into the pigpen, and called for their chopper. It came and the Battalion CO gave Captain Ervin some parting advice.

"Don't burn any hootches."

Zippo warfare was out; consideration was in . . . in the hearts and minds of the Saigon warriors.

Don't burn any hootches.

His chopper whisked him up into the sky.

A bullet tore a chunk of wood from the wall. Our side of the wall.

"Where'd that come from?"

"The village!"

"They're in the village!"

"There! That hut there!"

I lifted my rifle. Maybe I wouldn't nail the little bastard, but I could shake his aim.

"Don't shoot! Don't shoot! You'll hit our own men."

They were in our line of fire, just beyond the huts, fighting the NVA outside the village.

They'll get us. Hell, they've got us, if we don't fight back.

"Don't shoot! Killer, get us some support."

"Fire mission, over."

Another bullet hit inside the pen. A splinter cut my cheek. I felt the warm blood. Woodchips sprinkled over me. The sniper must have been as scared as me, his aim was so shaky. Another inch and . . .

We've got to break a platoon free and bring it back through.

A jet unloaded its rockets on the other side of the village.

"Where's that goddamned fire mission?"

"Here it comes."

We hear the first shell . . . coming right at us. Damn! We ducked. A fragment struck the wall.

"Hey, Killer, too close a little."

"Hell, no, it isn't. Bring it closer, Killer. Keep their heads down."

"One, this is Four. We need a dust-off. Over."

"Four, what do you have?"

"One that can't wait."

Captain Ervin spoke to the RTO on the Battalion net.

"Call the CO. We've got some whiskeys here. I want him to get a dust-off. . . . Four, we're bringing in a dust-off. Get your whiskeys back to us."

Another splinter was knocked from the wall.

"The dust-off wants to know what it's like down here," the RTO said.

We were at the only place he could land.

"It's cool. Tell him everything's cool."

Two soldiers supporting a third came running toward us . . . into the cross fire. They went down.

"Here comes the chopper."

The wounded crawled to us.

"Jesus!"

The dust-off landed. The enemy had so many targets they didn't know where to shoot first. WHAM! An RPG went off. The whiskey on his feet was knocked down.

"You hit?"

"Uh-uh. I mean, not again, I guess."

He had a compress on his shoulder and he was pale. Blood trickled

across his chest. I recognized him. He was the soldier who had asked me
if the Wolfhounds used dum-dum bullets in Korea.

"Good-bye. Good luck."

He ran to the chopper. The chopper rose. The AKs fired. The first
platoon disengaged and swept back through the village, bombing all suspect hootches (and all hootches were suspect). Smoke billowed into the
sky.

"CO's on the horn," the RTO said.

We could all hear his voice through the handset.

"Who fired those hootches? I ordered you not to set fire to any
hootches. Who did it? I want his name. I want the burning stopped. Do
you read me? Over."

Another hootch went up.

"Uh, Six, be advised," Captain Ervin said, "the fire was set by tracers
coming from inside the hootches. Over."

"I don't care . . . uh . . . inside? Over."

"Affirmative."

"Out."

Another caught fire; once they catch, they go like a torch. Maybe the
fire trapped the VC and burned them alive (we could hope), but, at the
least, the heat drove them into their tunnels. We breathed again. Captain
Ervin stood up.

"Okay, then . . ."

Lopez burst from the bunker.

"Don't leave me!"

He saw us.

"Oh."

He had fallen asleep and dreamt that we had abandoned him.

"Okay," the CO said, "I'll leave you here and take some troops and go
secure the PZ. Lie low—you never know."

"Know what? They'll think we all di-died?"

Fat chance, I thought, the NVA are much too sly, but I plunked down
behind the pigpen wall and closed my eyes—to savor a moment of silence—and listened to echoes. *They're inside. Where'd that one come
from? Killer, fire mission.*

I opened my eyes. The troops were behind whatever cover there was.
The people were down in their bunkers. Not even a chicken was scratching in the open. In the distance the slicks arrived and left. I could have
been alone, abandoned like my medic in his dream.

CRACK!

A grenade.

"Get him! Get the son of a bitch!"

Another grenade exploded and someone ripped off a belt on his M-60. I heard a scream.

"We got him! We got him!"

He lay there, face down, a poor little NVA grunt who had heard the sound of the receding rotors and believed that all the bad guys had gone away and he could stroll into the village. A G.I. shook his head.

"There's always that ten percent."

The villagers came out of their bunkers and gathered around the body. A sergeant tried to push them back.

"I don't want to see them crying over the little bastard," he said.

A mama-san—she could have been the kid's old grannie—stared at the body. Blood-red betel-nut juice oozed between her teeth and splattered her chin. She sucked in a glob and spit on the corpse. Her husband —if he was her husband—kicked the boy.

"They don't like them much, do they?" a G.I. said.

Chapter 13

I HAVE A RESTLESS NIGHT

Sunny arrested a number-one suspect. The suspect had no ID, he was old enough to be an Arvn, but he wasn't, and, if he wasn't an Arvn, then might he not be a VC? That was a question he couldn't answer, so we took him with us. He whined all the way to the PZ, he whined when we chucked him into the chopper, and he whined in the sky.

"Let's pitch this sucker out," someone said.

That was advice I wanted to take, but we didn't know he was VC and I was the S-5, in charge of hearts and minds, and the local farmers were less willing to give us their hearts and minds when bodies from above splashed into their rice paddies; then, too, prisoners sometimes have useful information. (Not this one, however; he was painstakingly interrogated by the spooks—whack! thump! crack!—and the result? Zilch. He was so retarded, he didn't even know there was a war on—not even the VC wanted him—so the spooks spread salve on the welts and burns, bandaged the lacerations, gave him a shot of penicillin, and sent him home—"Go back to your hamlet, van Dum, and remember always . . . we are your friends.")

He was lucky. If I had been faced with the same decision the next day, he might have met with an unfortunate accident, but that was the next day, this was today. We let him whine, and bounced along together, while I was thinking: Let's ride the sky forever, it's too scary on the ground, not to mention that the odds of collecting metal escalated with every landing. How many more missions were we going to cram into the day? I thought it must be about noon, and, at a firefight a landing, we'd have to hit two, maybe three, more hamlets. Noon? I checked my watch.

Five o'clock.

Lopez looked a question.

"It's 1700," I yelled.

"Yeah," he said.

"I thought it was noon."

He nodded.

"Hours go like minutes in a firefight."

I had survived. The whole day. I was heading home. No more hamlets, no more contact. Safe.

Clang!

Metal whacked against the side of the chopper. The slick lurched to one side and dropped. Lopez and I looked at each other; his face was pale and frightened, and I guess mine was, too. The suspect wailed.

"You and me both, charlie."

The pilot became active. Stay up, baby, stay up. After a while—time enough to lose a quart of perspiration—it became obvious that we were not going to crash (not this time), but, as far as I was concerned, the clang was an omen: Don't have anything to do with any flying machines in any form except that one Freedom Bird back to The World. I tumbled out at Mahone like a ship-wrecked sailor—the earth seemed to move beneath my feet and I had trouble walking the short distance to TOC. On the way I passed the doc.

"How's the kid?" he asked.

"Man, it's a scare-and-a-half out there."

And hueys are the scariest of all.

"What are you doing here?" the operations officer in the TOC said. "You're supposed to go out with recon tomorrow."

The recon platoon was quartered in town.

"We'll get a huey back for you."

Another ride. I could already hear the chopper returning.

My medics. I had to collect Leonard and Lopez. What about my dinner? I had to get information. I had to . . . The chopper was landing. I ran, and, as I ran, I yelled, "Lopez! Leonard!"

They were old soldiers. In the few moments we were on the ground, they had nosed out an open mess, grabbed a paper plate full of food— burned milk and meat, tomatoes and bread on the side—and downed it, filled up their plates again, got one for me, and somehow sensed that the chopper was meant for us—to take us to town—and beat me to the PZ. As for me, I had my rifle, I had grenades, I had the clothes on my back, I was field ready, ready to go . . . and ravenous. I looked at the food the two medics had.

"This is for you, sir," Lopez said, and handed me a plate filled with a semi-solid substance looking like a specimen of the Big Squirt.

Delicious. I sat in the door of the chopper, dangled my feet in the breeze, and ate. All in all, I had to confess, things could be worse. We could be flying into danger. We could be spending the night in the boonies. We could be hungry. Scared. Shot.

Instead we were going to the Big City. Dau Tieng. Civilization. I walked by buildings, some two stories high, constructed of brick and mortar and planks of wood, not rows of sandbags. I passed a swimming pool. Three of my friends, among them Lt. Artman, were taking a swim.

"Swimming," I said. "I'm out in the boonies getting my butt shot off and you're swimming."

Did they feel guilty? They laughed.

"Go get a beer and join us. The water's great."

They were listening to the radio: The Armed Forces Network. A reporter, Little Mary Sunshine, was interviewing patients in a hospital.

"How's it going, soldier?"

"Bad . . . uh . . ."

"Yes, and next to him I see . . . ah . . . sergeant? . . . yes, Sergeant Smith? And how you doing, sergeant?"

"My leg . . . a frag . . ."

"And over here we have another soldier-boy. What happened to you, young man?"

"A booby trap. It . . ."

"And here [desperate now, because she had been told to keep it light] we have a soldier who's sitting up in bed and smiling. You don't look so bad, young man. How's it going?"

"Fine. This is just as good as an R&R."

"You like it then?"

"Heck yeah. I don't see why everybody says it's so bad over here."

"Are they treating you all right?"

"Can't beat the service."

"That's the spirit. How did you get injured?"

"Oh, a bunch of us in the MAC-V replacement depot got up a football team and it's a pretty good one, too. One of the guys played some ball in college, but anyway, I was running and I got hit and tore some ligaments."

"Ooh, that must hurt."

"Yeah, some, but what the heck, I'm having a good rest and the doctor says I can leave tomorrow and I want to get back to my outfit."

"You like an active life?"

"You bet. In high school . . ."

I said, "I'm going to the mess hall and eat."

Nothing like fresh air and exercise (and good health) to whet the appetite. After a plate of spaghetti I went to our O Club and I was drinking a beer, thinking about the day that had been and the day that was coming, how wrung out I was—physically and emotionally wrung out, strung out, zomboid—when the first mortar round hit. I was in the bunker before the second round exploded. Fragments struck the wall. The NVA were retaliating for our mission in the rubber plantation. Another round and another fell—dozens of rounds—I had never heard so many explosions in my life.

"Medic! Medic!"

There was panic in the voice. I ran outside. A man was down, his blood spurting in the air. Three of his friends, drenched with blood, were trying to stop the bleeding with a tourniquet. By the time I reached them, it was too late, he had no more blood to bleed. One of them said to me, "He'll be okay. He'll be okay."

They were just average young Americans and they had tied the tourniquet around the wrong leg. Their friend was dead.

"Any of you hit?" I asked.

"No."

"Get under cover. There may be another attack."

"What about Jeff?"

"There's nothing you can do . . ."

Let the dead bury the dead.

". . . we'll get him later."

If it's happened, it's happened. Forget it. Go on. If you don't, you'll go crazy, because it can happen, right now, to those you know, or to you. My friends at the pool were walking back to our area when the mortar attack began.

"We were right in the middle. Rounds were exploding everywhere, coming closer. We hit the ditch. You know how some say clear the area and some say hit cover, and we were in that ditch and there was a bunker and it was like—I don't know—like someone whispered, run, and I ran and I got to the bunker and another one went off and knocked me inside and got me in the arm—I didn't even know I was hit—but, Christ, it must have landed right on top of them, and I would have stayed in the ditch, but something told me to run."

And that's the way it happened. Lt. Artman was dead.

I saw him just an hour ago.

The tears came.

He can't be dead.

I had been so close to the enemy I had heard the bolts slide back and forth in their rifles; he had been there, as safe as a man could be, in-country.

(Nobody expected me to get married, Lt. Artman said. My wife said even she was surprised when I showed up at the altar, but being married is great. When I get home . . .)

Later I tried to sleep. I closed my eyes and saw a woman with blood between her teeth. I looked at my watch. I closed my eyes again. I thought I heard a bolt snick closed. I touched my rifle. What was the name of the hamlet I'd been in?

When I arrived in-country, I had a fantasy—blast away a gook machine gun nest, save my platoon, receive a wound, perhaps a broken arm—a sling is romantic—win a DSC, rotate home, a hero's welcome.

My father had commanded a training company in Michigan during World War I. One of the recruits didn't want to go to France and die. The evening before Thanksgiving, when he was supposed to be on leave, he went into the boiler room, into the jungle of superheated pipes. He stuffed a rag into his mouth so that his involuntary cries of pain, when he insinuated himself in and around the steam pipes, wouldn't give him away. Then he cut his wrists. Five days passed before he was discovered. My father had to supervise the removal.

I could understand it—if the rest of my life was going to be like this single day, I'd prefer to get it over with.

(Well, I'd rather not be here, Lt. Artman said, but as long as I am, I'll do my job. That doesn't mean that I'll volunteer to be a hero. That's for you infatuated types.)

No one would wake me up and lead me to the PZ; if I said I overslept, no man could say I hadn't. I probably wouldn't go before a court. I might even be transferred to a safer job.

I was on the PZ at dawn.

Perhaps the lift won't come. Perhaps we'll have a quiet day. I stared at my boots. The recon lieutenant was in a chatty mood.

"I was talking to them just yesterday."

"Yes."

"Rear area jobs like theirs, you never know."

"No."

"Sitting at the pool."

"Yes."

"Having another brew and bang!"

"Yes."

"A job like theirs."

"Yes."

"If you're gonna get it, you're gonna get it."

"Yes."

"Makes you think though."

"Yes."

"But that's what I believe—if you're gonna get it, you're gonna get it."

"Yes."

"Doesn't keep me from ducking though."

"No."

"At least we're not the first lift."

"No."

I wasn't the only one feeling mortal that day. Lopez overslept and I didn't blame him a bit. He and Leonard had been assigned to S-5 because they had done their time on line and then some. S-5 was supposed to be safe, worthwhile duty, not flying into the boonies and delivering babies under fire.

"It doesn't make sense, sir," Leonard said. "Not if we've got to fight. We're supposed to pacify. How can we pacify if we're fighting?"

"Maybe today will be different."

The artillery was prepping the PZ. Lord, don't let the lift come, Lord, don't let the lift come, Lord, don't let the lift come, but it always comes, so take a deep breath, a long, slow breath. What happens, happens. Relax.

I felt the slight disturbance in the air, not yet a sound, but waves from an object far away beating against the air and then I heard the pulse of the rotor blades and saw the slicks themselves and thought—bumblebees can't fly.

They touched down and I ran forward.

Chapter 14

LET THE DEAD BURY THE DEAD

The floor of the huey was pocked with holes and littered with empty cartridge cases. The LZ was hot. So what else was new? The huey lifted. Then it settled back to the ground. The door gunner tapped me on the shoulder and pointed at the pilot. I leaned over.

"Sorry," the pilot yelled. "No can do."

"All right."

I spoke to the lift.

"We're going to have to find another slick."

"I don't like this," Leonard said.

"I don't blame you," I replied. "Let's go."

The door gunner of the second slick was kicking the empty cartridge cases out.

"Hot LZ?" I asked.

"Tee-tee," he said.

"You see," I said, though what I saw I couldn't say.

We were yanked into the air and hurtled to an LZ that had a pall of smoke of different colors over it. It looked hot to me. I leaped from the huey and dove into the dirt. I low-crawled for cover and low-crawled right into Captain Rubino's jungle boots. Captain Rubino, Bravo Company, CO for this day's flag-raising and pacification, was on his feet.

"Going somewhere?"

"Isn't the LZ hot?"

"Tee-tee," his killer said.

"When you're coming in and you see a couple of choppers burning on the ground," Captain Rubino added, "that's a hot LZ."

(On this LZ, because of my derring-do, if that's the word, I was given the nickname, Captain Marvel, the Flying S-5.)

We approached the hamlet across an open field which didn't have cover enough for a cowering mouse and I waited for the AKs and waited and gripped my rifle so hard my hands hurt . . . until I saw children running toward us. When the villagers play, the VC are away.

The villagers hadn't seen an Occidental since the French. A scruffy little ragamuffin tugged at my jacket.

"Donnez-moi chop-chop."

"Beat it, baby-san."

He did, to get some advice, and then he came back in translation.

"Gimme chop-chop."

I gave him a Tropic Bar. A Tropic Bar looks like a candy bar; it's the color of chocolate and it doesn't melt. (What has to be done to chocolate so it doesn't melt?)

The boy looked at it, sniffed it, and dropped it on the ground. In our own hamlet, where the children had come to know us, they would pitch the Tropic Bars back at us.

"Number ten G.I.!"

One great relief for me was that recon was going along to sweep the hamlet—no more walking alone and exposed into the middle of the unknown. Still, life was quieter under Bravo Company. Partly, it was style. Captain Rubino's style was: Okay, Charlie, I'm here now, so if you know what's good for you, you will clear the area. Partly it was luck and partly, maybe, the NVA had decided not to shoot into hamlets anymore.

I had a chance to look the hamlet over—it had a schoolhouse (école) with desks and benches. Some kid had carved his name on the desk, other kids had carved this or that, and one had carved a picture of a VC shooting down a helicopter. I think I know where these people stood.

The brass arrived. The major started a speech.

BANG!

We went to the ground, but my ear was already practiced enough to know that a couple of VC had just loosed off a few rounds and ducked. Half a dozen grenades. M-16s. A belt of M-60. Killer brought in a few rounds of artillery. A gunship shot a rocket or two.

Captain Rubino was already back on his feet, but I had found a nice little hole, no mud, no sharp rocks—it's amazing how now, wherever I was standing, there was a nice little hole available, and this hole was a particularly nice hole.

"You can get up now," Captain Rubino said to me.

"I think I may spend the rest of my tour here," I said, but I got up.

"Poor Charlie," Leonard said. "He pops a few caps and the whole world comes down on him."

We finished our business and moved to the PZ. It was quiet ("Too quiet," I could hear John Wayne say); we had to split the lift and we knew there were NVA around. The first lift went out; charlie now had his best chance. . . . I stood beside a clump of bushes—good concealment, lousy cover—and checked my route to the choppers. My lift crouched behind me. There were two paths through the brush. The slicks were returning. Eeny, meeny . . . right or left . . . I ran right. As I ran, something on the left, reflecting the sun, caught my eye—a wire—but the lift was following me and we were the last to leave, so the wire didn't really matter, but Jesus!—a wire where I might have gone.

I got on the radio immediately and informed the whole net that there was a wire on the edge of the field. At the next evening meeting in TOC I again mentioned the wire and furnished map coordinates. I specifically told the recon platoon leader about it, since he sometimes operated in that area. Then I heard nothing more, until one day I ran into him and asked him if he'd ever checked the field.

"Oh yeah."

"Find the wire?"

"Yeah."

"Nothing to it?"

"It was connected to a 105 shell."

But done is done, the past can't hurt you, and another hamlet was looming before me. According to the chopper radio it was quiet; I left the slick standing upright and I was walking with my head high. As it happened, just out of my sight, a little old man, who only wanted to avoid trouble, jumped on his bike and pedalled furiously away. The code states: Don't flee unless you wicked! Speedy, a platoon leader, yelled at him to stop.

He pedalled faster, but not fast enough to outrun Speedy's bullet; it struck the old man in the back, pierced a lung, and came out the front. He fell off his bike. (I hit the ground before he did—though halfway down I had realized that the shot was friendly.) We carried the old man to the central collection point and dumped him: He was hugging himself, holding himself together—grey pallor, clammy skin, depressed demeanor.

"That sucker's gonna be gone in ten, twenty minutes."

After the death of Lt. Artman, the death of the American boy in the street, after what I had been through, I wanted the old man to die, and everyone in the hamlet with him, but I had a job to do and letting the villagers watch a harmless old man die from an American bullet would not win hearts and minds, so I bundled him into the brass's loach, while they made their speeches, and sent him to a hospital. (I saw him months later in the hamlet. He lifted his dirty shirt and showed me a jagged scar; as far as I could tell from his snaggle-toothed grin, he bore us no grudge. If your neighbor's a tiger, expect to be scratched.)

After I saw the old man off, and the brass had spoken, I delivered an inspirational lecture, held a medcap, patted some baby-sans, hoisted the flag, and fini, di-di. As we were leaving, a huey, circling the hamlet on the look-see for NVA, found one, and he happened to be a marksman. The huey crashed. Leonard took off on the run.

"Hey, wait," I yelled.

Damn fool.

A gunship unleashed suppressing fire in all directions; we ran through the ricochets. A slick set down and everyone, door gunners and pilots, ran toward the wreck, but Leonard got there first and pulled out the crew. The downed chopper was already aflame. Then we arrived. "Get the machine guns," the recon leader said. Belts of ammunition were exploding. Recon ripped the guns out and we cleared the area. In minutes the huey looked like a heap of burned match sticks. The two-day airmobile pacification blitz was over.

Di-di, G.I. Di-di, MF.

PART VI

On the Wire

(January–February 1969)

Tropic Bars

The U.S. Army
Has decreed
The Tropic Bar
Is what we need.

It doesn't cost
A single cent,
Courtesy—
Our Government.

Doesn't melt
And doesn't run,
Doesn't doo-da
On your gun.

Spread your lips
And hold your nose;
Look out, taster,
In it goes.

Chomp it once
And chomp it twice,
Spit it out
And call the mice.

Looks like chocolate,
Smells like shit;
They won't even
Try a bit.

Lift your boot
And stomp the mice;
Compared to TBs,
They taste nice.

Chapter 15

WIVES AND CHILDREN

We captured the wife of a VC district chief and sent her to Brigade, Brigade sent her to Division, Division sent her to MAC-V, MAC-V consulted its computer and on 5 January sent her back down the line to us: "Take her to her village and identify her husband."

(Madam, would you be so kind as to point out your man?

There he is.

The one with the straw hat and sandals?

Yes, that's him.

Bang!)

She arrived in the evening with her baby and I was assigned to watch her through the night and then guide her to Ben Chua, where we would see what was what.

We were eating dinner when the first mortar round hit. By the time the second arrived I was in the bunker and I hadn't spilled a drop of the slop on my plate. My team was right behind me . . . but not the woman. What was she waiting for—John Wayne? Admittedly, if he had been with a woman who didn't know enough to come in out of the attack, he would have grabbed her, hauled her to the door of the bunker, and thrown her inside. Of course, the woman would have been Maureen O'Hara, and that might have made a difference, though I doubt that I would have noticed even Maureen O'Hara in her prime once the mortars began to hit, and, anyway, this woman was not a movie star and neither was I, and I had to consider whether or not to risk my neck for a female VC.

I had to.

I stuck my head out and yelled, "Lie day, mama-san."

She had only been waiting for an invitation.

When the mortars let up, we emerged, except for the woman (her name was Prudence) and we found the Permanent Private cavorting around with a piece of shrapnel clasped in his hand.

"Look at the heroes," he jeered. "Run into the bunker. I stayed out here. I'm not afraid. This hit right here. But the heroes run to the bunker."

Too right. And when the NVA fired an encore to catch those of us who had emerged to look after the wounded, I ran again and I didn't bother about my dinner this time. The second salvo was also too much for the Permanent Private; he came after me. Kirksey grabbed his shirt.

"No way, man. You like it so much, you stay out there."

Duty can be distasteful, but I had to intervene.

"Let him in, Kirksey."

Then we heard the call, "Medic! Medic!"

Kirksey ran out of the bunker to help. Kirksey may have wanted to go his own way—and the Army doesn't accept that—but he had guts and he was a leader. Chico and Touchberry were at the wounded man's side already, cutting his clothes off. He had punctures up the kazoo.

"Jesus," Chico said, "were you going for a record? You're going to have a permanent leak. The Human Sprinkler."

"Yeah," the wounded man said, "they sure nailed me."

"We'll need at least a hundred bandaids."

The victim looked at himself with interest.

"You missed a couple."

I could hardly believe how composed he was. Neither could one of the sidewalk superintendents.

"Jeez, he's hit bad. Is he going to make it?"

The whiskey flopped over on his back.

"I'm hit bad," he moaned.

"Hell," Touchberry said and pushed an IV into him.

I had a restless night. We were mortared again and the woman was in the bunker with me and while I doubted that she would try to slit my throat, nevertheless, I did not sleep well.

We left the wire before dawn and we walked down the road to Ben Chua, a hamlet famous for its VC rallies. The point was tense. On the outskirts of the hamlet, in half-darkness, the point fired. I could see the muzzle flash. Even as I was going down, I thought, *right into a mud puddle. Where did mud come from, in the dry season? Why was I going down, when an M-16 had fired?* Splash.

The villagers were wary, we knew the NVA was nearby. I gave a speech to the collected villagers and then I asked the woman, "Which is your husband?"

"He's not here," she replied.

"Not here? Where is he then?"

"In jail."

"In jail?"

"You arrested him a month ago."

Why you dumb broad . . .

"Why didn't you tell us that?"

"You didn't ask."

And she actually thought, now that she had done what we wanted, we would let her go. We hauled her back to prison.

In revenge for the visit, the NVA mortared our FSB and we retaliated with a fire mission on the suspected location of their base camp. I stayed up to listen to the guns. It gave me a peculiar feeling to hear them fire and then to hear the muted rumblings of the exploding shells in the distance. After the fire mission I went to my cot. Moments later Kirksey woke me.

"There's someone out beyond the wire calling to us."

I got up.

"G.I., G.I., help, help."

A flare showed three human shapes, one supported by the other two.

"I'm not ordering anyone to go out," the CO said.

"What the hell," a medic named Redd said, "I'll go."

He found a twelve-year-old boy with his scalp blown over his face, his body burned, and a leg ripped open.

Our artillery.

We had shot at a suspected enemy base camp, but had we hit a hamlet? The next morning a patrol went out to investigate and found both a hamlet and some NVA. During the fight three panic-stricken children ran into the crossfire. A sergeant yelled, "Cease fire! Cease fire!"

Our troops stopped firing. The sergeant waved at the children.

"Lie day, goddammit to hell, you little bastards, lie day."

The NVA were not sentimental. Their bullets hit one of the children. He folded up into a little bundle in the middle of the field. The other two escaped. We called for napalm.

"Fry the bastards."

The NVA considered Ben Chua theirs; we considered it a particularly fruitful hunting ground and we ambushed it regularly. Every day we made contact.

"We were in the huts on the fringe of Ben Chua," a noncom told me. "I'm looking out over an open area and there were three figures walking toward me. Broad daylight. I thought they must be U.S., coming like that across an open field, but I kept watching, and they were dressed in khaki.

" 'Christ,' I say, but I'm not going to blow this one. 'Let them get close. Nobody fire until I do,' I say.

"I figured we could get all three, but as they get closer, they start to fan out. Professionals. I level at the one in the middle. I have it on full auto, but I take a good sight picture and when he's about seventy-five meters away, I let fly. Pow! He goes down."

First report was that he had shot an NVA general, but a closer examination of the body revealed a sad truth—he had killed an NVA tiwi, that is, an NVA second lieutenant.

Our AO was hot and getting hotter. To make matters worse, the four hamlet chiefs, and the chiefs' chief, the five we had chosen when we first arrived, now returned to us. (I was appointed their guardian angel.) They were fresh from Arvn school and eager to show what they had learned: Gerrymandering, taxation, minor thuggery. Their influence, to be sure, was limited because they had to live in Mahone, where the NVA could not pay a personal call on them; the NVA, nonetheless, did welcome them.

"Hey, fireflies," Kirksey said on the night of 8 January 1969.

"Fireflies?"

"There."

He pointed at the hamlet, where, sure enough, we could see dozens of luminous specks. Redd laughed.

"Reminds me, when I was first in-country, I saw some fireflies and I thought they were aiming stakes for mortars."

We heard a noise—plop—like a foot pulled from mud. Lots of noises. Our mascot put his tail between his legs and scuttled into the bunker.

"Fireflies hell! Those ARE aiming stakes."

"IN-COMING!"

We were in the bunker before the first round exploded; fragments hit the blast wall. As always I had two immediate thoughts; first, thank heaven I'd made it to the bunker, and, second, thank God I wasn't in the Artillery. Infantry can hunker in a bunker until the mortar attack is over, but the redlegs have to man their guns to shoot a counterbarrage, in this case, HE and flachette, zero elevation, point-blank at the village. Some of the hootches caught fire. We popped flares. Shadows danced between the huts and we fired at them with everything we had. If the NVA had intended to assault, they changed their minds.

In the morning's sweep we found nary a sign of the NVA. The children came out for chop-chop, the prostitutes were gathered under their tree, all was as usual, except the hamlet was a smoking ruin and the inhabitants were not pleased—so far the NVA's scheme had been successful. Sunny had to harangue the whining multitude:

We're sorry your village got creamed and we will help you rebuild what was blown away, but, doggone it, folks, you can't let the VC come right into your backyard and shoot at us with mortars.

Two water buffalo had been wounded; the poor beasts oozed blood with every breath they took. I had once wondered, when I read *All Quiet on the Western Front,* how soldiers could be affected by the sight of a wounded horse and so callous toward wounded men (enemy, of course); now seeing these poor dumb brutes awaiting death I felt a sympathy for them I knew I could never feel for dead or wounded NVA.

The beasts were going to die and it was our fault, or, at least, our steel, and you can't go around knocking off a farmer's water buffalo—his wife, his children, burn down his hootch, okay, he can replace them, but a water buffalo is valuable and so, after I had investigated and certified that the U.S. Artillery was to blame, I handed over compensation in cash, fifty bucks a buff (in pi), which is what we would have paid had we, in fact, knocked off a wife or child. (The villagers could not grasp our scale of values.) Once he was paid off, the farmer butchered the animals and transported one carcass to town to sell.

At the evening briefing the intelligence officer reported that he had heard a rumor there was going to be a VC-NVA rally and barbecue that night in Ben Chua. We didn't receive an invitation, but we decided to go anyway.

We sent a company. It was to set up a cordon on the south of the hamlet, but sometime in the middle of the night, for whatever reason, Battalion ordered it to move.

Move?

At night?

Only the enemy moves at night, but there our company was, moving hand on belt, through the moonless night. A G.I. in the middle of the column was seized by the arm. An angry voice from the dark demanded an answer . . . in Vietnamese.

"Jesus Christ, let go of me!" he cried and fired a magazine at the dark shape.

The shape screamed. Voices called all around, Vietnamese and English. NVA and Americans trying to figure out who was who. The column kept moving, went to earth, and formed a tight perimeter.

The NVA didn't know what they were dealing with—a platoon? a company? a battalion?—but the general situation was clear: This was a trap. They faded into the night.

When we swept into Ben Chua the next morning, we found no NVA, but we did find the remains of a barbecue, and a hamlet full of cele-brants. Villagers from Co Trach had come to eat buffalo and see the VC and NVA, but now, with us there, they were beginning to have second thoughts. Two young boys tried to sneak away on their bicycles. Sunny yelled at them and fired a couple of warning shots. The boys stopped. Then we had to decide what to do with them. We could have sent them to Dau Tieng. We could have shot them, for that matter, but Thi, a girl from Co Trach, approached me.

Thi was a young girl, mid-teens, not unattractive, of a well-to-do family. She spent a lot of time at our medcaps, watching Leonard, and giggling and blushing; otherwise, she was intelligent and she picked English up quickly.

Thi said to me,

"Please, captain, they are boys."

"Do you know them?"

"Yes."

I talked to the Spook.

"Do you think they're VC?"

"Not really, but they probably will be in a couple of years."

"What do you want to do?"

"I don't know. Throw a good scare into them."

"How about this? We've got a good contact in Thi. We can use this to build her up in the village. We can make it clear to them, and to her, that we are letting them go because of her."

So we let them go.

We had worked hard to establish ourselves here. When we arrived the whole village was VC. Now—though there were still many VC—there were many people who (dare I put it so strongly?) liked us. The children found our presence exciting and profitable—candy, clothes, games, weapons, action—and they were learning English. Thi was a contact (a completely unwitting contact), and, as she was young and attractive, I did not think she would be a target for assassination. Some of the adults conversed with me, mostly with the help of an interpreter, but they learned to greet us in English, "Hello, daiwi."

And I tried to reciprocate.

"Chao ong, mon joy. Chao co, mon joy."

They were beginning to believe that the VC were through. We seemed to be everywhere and we seemed to be there to stay. The VC had to sneak into their own village at night—and they ran a desperate risk of ambush or betrayal when they did. Any one of their neighbors, even their own children, might inform on them. Moreover, the mortar attack which had provoked our retaliation had turned the villagers against them. We were "winning their hearts and minds."

We had also carried out our tactical mission to interdict the NVA supply lines. We had now stayed over two months, but the pickings were so good that Brigade decided we should stay longer, until the NVA control of the area was completely broken. Unfortunately, because of the original conception, a three-day mission, Mahone had been established at the extreme range of Brigade artillery and too far down the road to resupply by Battalion's resources alone. Brigade was forced to commit the balance of its resources in air support and mechanized troops to keep us going.

For tactical reasons, then, Brigade decided to move us closer to Dau Tieng. We were ordered to move Battalion up the road a few miles to Ben Tranh, but to leave behind a company-sized fort at Mahone (under Captain Ervin—"God, it's lonely here!"). Soon, however, that fort, too, was closed down.

When it was, the NVA proclaimed a victory—they had driven us away.

"You see," they said, "the Americans will not protect you. They will not stay. They will leave. But you will stay . . . and so will we."

They forced Thi to go to the NVA basecamp and cook their meals and wash their clothes and confess her errors in sessions of self-examination. She was not maltreated, but she could have been and she knew it. When I saw her again, she had become shy. I didn't blame her. Others were corrected in harsher fashion.

Our reasons for moving were tactically sound, but the move lost us the people of Co Trach.

Chapter 16

BLUE BLIMPS AND SWEAT HOGS

Colonel Reese had wanted the next Wolfhound Fire Support Base to be called "Fire Support Base Damron," after one of our lieutenants who had been killed in action, but Colonel Reese was gone, and the powers who name bases preferred the Confederate general Mahone (again) to a lowly Wolfhound lieutenant. Our new fire support base was called Mahone II. Nonetheless—and I hope the reader will excuse me—I am going to perpetrate a fiction and call Mahone II Fire Support Base Damron.

Damron was across the road to the east of Ben Tranh (a pleasant village on the edge of the rubber plantation); to the south of Damron was the plantation house; west of the plantation house and south of Ben Tranh was Ft. Rebel. Ft. Rebel had been put in place to watch Ben Tranh and to guard the road.

While the fort was being built, G.I.'s had paid the children of Ben Tranh one candy bar for every five sandbags they filled. In the process the kids picked up English, as they demonstrated when a visitor from a mech unit asked a Wolfhound, "How can you stand to have all these gook kids around so close?"

"Hey," one of the kids said, "you no call me gook, you G.I. son of a bitch!"

I had run a few medcaps in the village and been shot at. As we learned later, the NVA had instructed the VC to keep an eye on us from the brush, note everything we did, and not engage us, but one couldn't resist the temptation.

We had also had a series of skirmishes while establishing Damron.

One morning, as I was walking into the hamlet, Madam Fred—the prostitutes had moved with us—waved at me.

"Bad!"

"Bad?"

What have we done now?

"Numba ten, daiwi!"

She pointed at the root of a tree. An unexploded round from an M-79 grenade launcher was lying there. The M-79 round, when fired from a launcher, rotates. The rotation arms the fuse, which then goes off on impact. If the round should hit a tree before it has been armed, it can bounce back (still spinning and arming) and explode in the face of the person who fired it. An unexploded round lying on the ground was death postponed.

"Okay," I said, "I'll call an Engineer."

Only a fool takes unnecessary chances.

"Bad!" Madam Fred repeated and, before I could stop her, picked it up and tossed it aside. There are a thousand stupid ways of getting killed and she had found a good one, but the round didn't go off.

I gave a medcap to sullen and suspicious people and I returned to our fire support base. Damron was plush. We had electricity—TVs, stereos, hot food. We had enclosed commodes, piss tubes, and Australian shower heads. And our TOC (Tactical Operations Center) was air-conditioned— one day, while Speedy was driving through division base, he saw an air-conditioner attached to a general's house trailer; he stopped, he knocked, he received no answer, and we acquired a prime air-conditioning unit.

What a relief to come out of the torrid heat of the sun into the cool of the TOC. Sure, one day on the counter I noticed a sticky brown soup that had once been a box of chocolates, but I don't care, the TOC felt cool and we sought excuses to drop in and linger. The chaplain, who had been advised by Brigade to make regular visits to the field—overnight visits— came to TOC and explained that he was a transient, no fixed abode, and therefore . . .

Outside, bum!

He was not a popular guy. Once he had denounced porno flicks.

"If you find any," the XO said, "let me take a look at them."

"If I find any more," Captain Crux said, "I will see the Brigade commander."

The chaplain—wiser heads advised—was just doing his job, but, nonetheless, he was bounced from TOC and he had to seek sanctuary in the aid station. There, however, he saw the doctor's Playboy centerfold, he denounced it, he counselled him on the deleterious effects pornography has on the morale of the men, he reminded him of his duty both as officer and Battalion surgeon, and then he asked, "Do you have room for me to stay here?"

"No."

He found a home with Charlie Company, but he had to leave when he heard a description of a fraternity game called Dog. Dog is a kind of panty raid with the girls still inside the panties.

Bravo's commander—Captain Rubino—took him in.

"You can stay here, Padre, if you don't mind living with an unregenerate Catholic."

"We all do God's work, my son."

But it seemed that the chaplain with the Roman collar was going around the perimeter of Damron and he was filling three sandbags at every position.

"He is?"

That dirty . . .

The chaplain went off on his own rounds and had his assistant fill *four* sandbags at every bunker.

("Hey, let's get the rabbi out here.")

That was the chaplain. Nobody loved him, many thought he was a jerk, but nobody hated him, either . . . , that is, before he murdered his most faithful parishioner.

"If I have faith in God, will I come through this?" a soldier asked him.

Since the chaplain had no doubts, he told the soldier, "If you attend services regularly, if you read the Bible daily, if you have true and abiding faith, then you will survive."

Thus far the chaplain's hands were clean, because he had left a loophole, but he really wanted to nail down this conversion and so he used a concrete example. There was a pious individual (who read the Bible whether anyone was watching or not), by name . . . well, call him Fromm . . . and the chaplain said, "If you have true and abiding faith, you will survive, just like Specialist Fromm."

That afternoon a mortar round hit inside the bunker line and killed Fromm.

"I'm not a superstitious guy," Touchberry said, and he spoke for all of us, "but just the same, the chaplain killed Fromm."

Attendance at his services dropped off and he didn't understand why. He demanded that the CO order the men to attend. The CO refused. He appealed to higher authority.

"It's one damned thing after another," the CO said. "If they'd just let us get on with it, we could win this war, but we've got Congressmen and reporters and mothers and chaplains and we've got to see that the boys lead wholesome lives and nobody hurts their feelings and then I finally satisfy the chaplain and there're the Blue Blimps."

The first Blue Blimp I ever saw, I saw as I was walking in, and she was walking out, of Damron. Hey, I thought, when I was at a goodly distance, this looks like a woman, a dainty, delicate, little American woman. And, indeed, it was a woman, but as I got closer, she got bigger. Bigger and bigger. A Blue Blimp.

These sweet, wholesome all-American girls joined the Red Cross and came overseas to service (excuse me, I meant serve) our boys, raise their morale, and improve their morals by reminding them of what the war was all about: The girl they left behind.

They exuded innocence, though I don't believe that anyone could be as innocent as they seemed to be and I heard of one who certainly wasn't.

"Guess how much I earned last week?" she asked a friend of mine.

He had no idea how much Red Cross girls were paid and he told her so.

"Five thousand dollars."

"Five thousand dollars?"

"A general paid me five thousand dollars to spend the weekend with him."

"Five thousand dollars?"

"And he's going to help me convert it so I can get it home."

$5000.00? That was as much as I was paid in a year.

"I figure I can clear a hundred thousand dollars while I'm over here."

Twenty weekends.

"Of course, I can't expect to do that well every weekend."

"But doesn't it bother you?"

"Does it bother them? They just zip it up and walk away."

"But society, your parents, boyfriends?"

"Oh, I figure it'll take a year to clean out my mind after I get home but then I'll still have the hundred thousand."

Blue Blimps and Sweat Hogs. The title Blue Blimp had a certain justification to it, but Sweat Hog was simply a bum rap. Admittedly the nurses did not look like the actresses on M.A.S.H., but neither did they look like their army career was one last desperate grab for a man; still, we Americans are like that—the men who risked their lives in the boonies were Grunts and the nurses who did the dirty job of caring for the wounded were Sweat Hogs.

Every day I went into Ben Tranh. After the medcap I usually had a Coke. (50 cents per can—are there Coke-girl capitalists in the communist dream?) Redd played with the children, Kirksey talked with Slash and Madam Fred, and I teased what I called a possum fern, a little red plant that grows along the ground and has a leaf about the size of a fingernail. When touched, it shrivels up, turns brown, and plays dead, until the coast is clear (I don't know how a plant decides the coast is clear), and then it spreads out again.

The village was cool and pleasant and quiet . . . no Arvns. Redd decided to take a nap. Kirksey and a white G.I. sat on their helmets near me and talked. They were quite a sight, the huge black-bearded, black-skinned Kirksey and the slight, wan G.I.

"When I get back to The World," Kirksey said, "I ain't even gonna take no crap from the man no more."

"Say it, brother," the G.I. said.

"I'm gonna go home and look him in the eye."

"I was there, man, where were you?"

"Damn straight."

"The patriot back in his natal home."

"Huh!"

"I see it. A bar. Jukebox playing. Everybody inside rapping, till you walk in, Bogie cigarette."

"Jim Brown."

"Foxes check you out—who is that bad dude?"

"You got it, brother."

"The owner himself comes over."

"Yeah."

"Looks up at you."

"Yeah."

"Says, 'We don't serve niggers here.' "

Fire Support Base Damron (Mahone II)

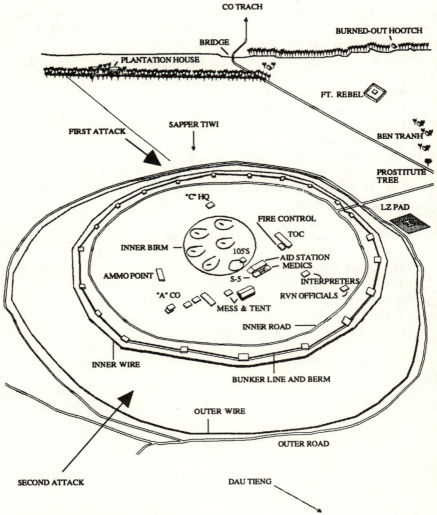

Prepared by Alfred S. Bradford

Chapter 17

NIGHT ATTACK

A story goes that once upon a time in some forgotten hamlet a VC handed a little girl a primed grenade and told her, Go give it to that American.

The American, to protect himself, shot the child.

I told this story to the Brigade S-5 when I was summoned to town to report on the local hearts and minds.

"I'd never shoot a child," he said.

Downy birds. They should wear a patch upon their chests, so those of us who want to live will know them: An ostrich, its head in the sand, surrounded by a Latin motto—*rara avis, vita brevis.*

But, the downy bird aside, the trips to town were fun. I could sit at a table under a roof and tell a native girl to fetch the food—"Baby-san, you bring G.I. chop-chop, okay?"

"Sir, do you mean you want your dinner?"

I could have a shower, go to the medics' hootch, have a beer, and watch the Army Network on TV. *Combat* was a favorite, and not so bad a show, for those who like it, though Sarge, the hero, must hold the record for Purple Hearts, and all the commercials were Army pitches. One, for example, stressed the evils of dope: Three sentries smoke a joint and then get greased.

This visit I saw a new commercial.

"Oh, here it is," a medic said and slily asked me, "Sir, you seen this one yet?"

No.

A soldier was preparing for the night. He inspected his mosquito bar and he sprayed the air with an insect bomb.

In-coming!

I hit the door.

"Wait, sir, wait, it's just the TV."

A dead mosquito (according to the army script) falls with a whistle like a mortar round.

Everyone in the room had been fooled at least once by the dying mosquito; all of them were prepared for the whistle (and my reaction), and still some of them followed me on my flight to the bunker, because the spine is quicker than the brain and the sight of a man running is completely persuasive. We were a bit tense.

I went to the O Club to have a beer to settle my nerves. I was drinking a beer with Bobby L (a company commander), Cash Flow (then a platoon leader), and Lt. Brown (a former platoon leader, now adjutant) and we were idly talking of this and that—how Cash was asked by an adviser if the NVA really had put a bounty on our heads ("Sure," Cash said, though that was the first he had heard of any bounty, "five hundred for an enlisted man and a thousand for an officer")—and Bobby L picked up his half empty can and squeezed it and we watched him and we saw the side bend—plink.

I started for the floor. So did Cash Flow. Halfway there, of course, we realized that the noise had come from the beer can and, somewhat shame-faced, we straightened up again.

"Jeez, guys," Bobby L said. "I'm sorry. I was even scared myself."

Lt. Brown raised his eyebrows.

"Guys?"

"It's been . . ."

. . . rough, I was going to say, but . . .

BANG!

As we crouched in the bunker, Lt. Brown said, "Oh, I know what that was, that was the five-inch gun. It fires a round every two minutes."

"Roger," we said.

We went back to the table.

BANG!

As we crouched in the bunker, Lt. Brown said, "Uh, gentlemen, that's the five-inch gun. It fires a round every two minutes."

"Roger."

We went back to the table.

BANG!

We started for the bunker, all of us except Lt. Brown, who flinched but kept his seat.

"Guys? The five-inch gun?"

We halted—yes, the five-inch gun—and resumed our seats.

BANG!

We came to our feet. Lt. Brown shook his head.

"You guys seem a little tense."

No kidding.

My cot was located in a room I shared with three of my fellow officers on the second floor of a picturesque old French mansion. Because I was a transient I had the spot farthest from the exit. I fell asleep immediately . . . and I woke running down the stairs.

What am I doing on the stairs?

I stopped.

Behind me a trio of soprano voices broke into a chorus.

"Keep going! Keep going! They're still coming in!"

Then I heard the explosions.

What with our artillery, mortar attacks, and TV commercials, I was ready to return to the quiet of Damron, but when I did return I found that Colonel Meredith had introduced a new idea. He believed in the ideal of the officer corps, gentlemen dedicated to the profession of arms, and, therefore, he instituted the dining-in.

Officers and Gentlemen should dine together in an evening mess served by the enlisted men. This dining-in would give us a sense of esprit and enhance our prestige. Captain Crux thought it was a great idea; the rest of us rather thought we were all in this together and we boycotted the mess tent. (Thus had we been trained by Colonel Reese.) The CO ordered us to eat there. We fetched our own trays. He ordered us to sit and be served. We went early to avoid him.

"As of tomorrow," he said, "we will dine at 1800 hours in clean fatigues and polished boots and if I have to have you stand parade, I will."

Colonel Meredith's style worked against him. He criticized the troops, who, when fired upon, instead of immediately returning fire, first took cover. Wrong! Return fire first, then take cover! He, himself, in the field would run to the sounds of small arms fire, to see what was what. He had guts, but neither officer nor enlisted man appreciated his courage; instead we thought he was a fool.

Perhaps he hoped that the dining-in would bring us together.

Three hours before dawn on 18 February I woke on the floor of my bunker with my right hand on my rifle and my left groping for my gasmask, grenades, and ammunition. The ground was shaking from the artillery (which fired directly over the top of my bunker) and from exploding mortars. I crawled to the door. In the wavering light of a flare I saw three figures running toward me. I raised my rifle and snapped the safety off.

Are they or aren't they? Flares distort what you see. So does fear. Be sure.

Americans.

But were they running to or were they running from? I caught up my satchel of ammunition and grenades and got to the inner perimeter, the aid station, and the artillery. The wounded were starting to come. The NVA were through the wire.

A sapper squad had cut the wire and fired an RPG (the NVA bazooka) directly into a bunker. All the Americans inside were killed except one. He was knocked cold and didn't recover consciousness until the NVA entered the bunker.

For a real thrill, try getting knocked out and then waking up with gooks running their hands over your face.

The NVA collected the rifles and searched the bodies.

They thought I was dead. Everyone else was.

The NVA had to destroy the guns or their assault would have no chance. They crouched outside the bunker, using it for cover, while one of them aimed an RPG at the artillery. A howitzer crew frantically tried to lower the barrel of their one-oh-five enough to shoot directly at the NVA. The muzzle wouldn't depress that far.

I had a grenade. I pulled the pin and held the handle down.

The Battalion CO had gathered some personnel from headquarters to make a counter-attack.

I dropped the grenade outside.

The colonel charged. The NVA pulled the trigger of the RPG. The grenade exploded. The RPG went off—off course—and the rocket almost tore Colonel Meredith's leg in half. The grenade killed the NVA.

Then I thought I'd take a little rest.

The sappers were dead, but more NVA were coming through the break in the wire and mortars were still hitting inside the fire support base. A company ammo dump blew up and scattered broken cannisters of CS gas; the wind blew the CS across the cut wire and the gas confused the enemy. They hesitated and lost direction. Their officers shouted at them, tried to regain control, but the surprise was gone and time had run out. They were caught in the wire. The 105s were levelled at them. The noise, the gas, the shock—they lost their heads. Orange tracers crisscrossed the dark confused huddle of the attackers. I could hear them screaming.

NVA in the tree line tried to provide covering fire, so the trapped men could escape, but our artillery shot flachettes directly at them, hundreds, thousands of darts. A helicopter fired a mini-gun. Its tracers drew a solid luminous line from sky to ground, hundreds of rounds in less than a second. The attack was broken, but the scattered firefight went on.

One of the wounded in the aid station became hysterical.

"Call a dust-off! We'll all be killed! Call a dust-off! Get me out of here!"

A fragment had pierced his upper arm.

Another man had his jaw blown off. If he went into shock, he would die. The panicky flesh wound was spooking him.

"Kirksey," the doctor said.

Kirksey put a massive hand on the wounded man's shoulder.

"Hey, man, be cool, or I'll put you out of here."

He shut up.

The doctor spoke calmly and patiently to the jaw wound.

"You're going to make it, son, no sweat. These days we can take a rib and build your jaw as good as new. I've seen it done. It's going to hurt and it'll take some time, but you'll be okay."

The colonel was brought to the aid station on a stretcher.

"I got them! I got them! I saved the bunker line!"

He was thinking medal of honor, and he was a brave man, and he had acted bravely, but the bravest man can be confused by pain and danger and noise.

"You did, sir," the sergeant major said, "you did. I saw it."

The sergeant-major had been hit in the head. I cleared the colonel's rifle. The rifle was jammed. Only one round had been fired. The G.I. in the bunker had saved us. Nevertheless, it's a fact of army life that colonels get the medals and privates clean the latrine.

The surgeon put the colonel out with a shot of morphine.

I never quite knew when the light changed from parachute flare to sun, but suddenly I realized it was day. The NVA had withdrawn and we could inspect the damage. Five NVA corpses were sprawled around the bunker. Their clothes were half blown off. A G.I. sightseer pointed at the anatomy thus revealed.

"Stiff dick the hard way."

Thin cloths were tied around their arms and legs to use as tourniquets: If they were hit hard in an arm or a leg they could twist the cloth and stop the bleeding.

There were twenty bodies on the wire. They looked like plastic dummies from the set of *The Green Berets*. We threw them in the garbage dump.

There were also dead Americans. They lay, covered by a tarp, on stretchers. A G.I., seeing them, turned away and wiped his eyes with his sleeve. Another soldier, passing by, asked if he could look at one of them.

"You think you know him?"

"Naw. I just never seen no one dead before."

Chapter 18

DOG FOOD

The night the NVA hit us, they also hit Brigade (and Division). What a mess! The rear base was unprepared, and, anyway, as a rule of thumb, the larger the base the worse the security, because the bunker line is manned with cooks and clerks, and cooks and clerks don't believe it can happen to them, and they don't know what to do when it does—some of them ran away, some of them froze and were killed on the spot. The firefight spilled over into our O Club.

Cash Flow was drinking a beer with some other lieutenants. Cash Flow had been the sergeant-major of line lieutenants, aggressive and daring (though his daring fell on the safe side of stupidity), before he got a letter from a lawyer: Congratulations! Your rich aunt has bequeathed you half-a-million dollars.

$500,000!

He thought about the things he wanted—a Maserati, a mansion, a cellar of wines, a beautiful woman, several beautiful women. He thought about the money and he thought about where he was. "God must be a practical joker," he said . . . and . . . "I've got to make it out of here." He became a nervous wreck. He smoked dope, popped pills, and chased the pills with alcohol—breakfast was usually a handful of darvons and a beer, lunch was a couple of joints and a beer, supper a few pills, and after supper he drank.

Eventually the new Battalion commander (The Bear) decided to save Cash Flow from himself and sent him back on line as a company commander, but at this time he was in the rear, at the Officers' Club, passed out in a chair . . . and the balloon went up. Red and green tracers criss-crossed the bar room. The beer drinkers were flat on their faces.

A mosquito couldn't have flown across that room, they said.

Cash woke up. He stared at his friends on the floor.

"Hey, guys?"

Some kind of game?

He saw luminous streaks of jade and vermilion caroming off the walls.

"Oh wow!"

He stood up.

Too much junk in the blood. Seeing colors dancing in the air.

"Time for bed."

He walked through the bullets up the stairs to his bed and there he slept the night away. While he slept, Lt. Gutierez was in his company area, under arrest. Two nights in a row Brigade staff had sent him out on ambush by the same route to the same site. When they gave him the same orders the third night, he protested. They explained that Staff gave the orders and lieutenants carried them out . . . or else. He needed no crystal ball to predict what would happen—the NVA would be there, waiting for him.

He led his troops into bunkers along the bunker line to spend the night, but a staff officer discovered him there and turned him in. (Hell hath no fury like a noncombatant.) Lt. Gutierez was awaiting a court-martial for cowardice in the face of the enemy, when the NVA broke through the bunker line. Armed only with a .45, he organized the defense of his area and then ran to the company ammo point. By himself, with his .45 and a few grenades, he beat off several enemy attacks.

Meanwhile, the largest group of NVA must have thought the battle was over, because they dress-right-dressed in a column of fours and marched down the airstrip . . . toward a row of armored personnel carriers armed with miniguns. At first the mech people thought that the NVA were G.I.'s because only Americans would be dumb enough to pull a stunt like that, but a sergeant took another look—"Them's gooks!"—and pulled the trigger.

Two hundred NVA died right there, and the attack was broken.

The commanding general of the 25th Division arrived, in person, to assess the situation. He learned about Lt. Gutierez's defense of the ammo point—saving the ammo point had certainly been one of the turning points of the battle—and the general threw his arm around Gutierez and said, "I want this boy to get a DSC."

"Oh, general," a local staff officer said, "we can't do that. He's facing a court-martial for cowardice in the face of the enemy."

"Bull shit," the general said.

From then on we called Gutierez *Hero.*

A few NVA had survived to hide in ditches and trees, and, for days afterwards, they sniped at pedestrians. The next time I came to town, I noticed that the Brigade S-5 (he had been sniped at from a ditch) had gone through a metamorphosis of vocabulary. The Vietnamese all had become gooks and they now deserved dark death.

The NVA also hit Division and Division was an even bigger mess than Brigade. Squads of NVA ran loose. They burned helicopters. They found staff officers asleep and cut their throats. Morale plummeted in the rear. The NVA, of course, never came close, or could come close, to a military victory over American troops, but they didn't have to, they only had to shake public confidence in us.

I went to the Arvn bunker to encourage the village officials. The village officials were not at home. They had learned of the coming attack from their own sources and had gone to cover in town the night before.

"They ever think of telling us?" the S-3 asked me.

"Not likely. And they haven't come back, either. I think that's a clue."

"Yeah."

We restrung the concertina, filled sandbags, rebuilt the bunkers, set out claymores, and cleared our fields of fire of enemy corpses (we threw them in the dump). We worked all day, had a quiet night—thank the Lord—and worked the following morning. By then the dead in the dump had attracted swarms of flies.

"It's as much as your life is worth to go near that place."

The flies were everywhere. You no sooner opened a can of C's—the kitchen had been knocked out—than the flies covered the food, flies fresh from their orgy at the dump. I waved them away, but like the NVA on which they fed—you are what you eat?—they kept on coming back. They had to fight a headwind to do it and I didn't have to smell the bodies while I ate, but, unfortunately, the detail that burned out the crappers was doing it upwind and a cloud of odoriferous black smoke hung above me, dripping black ash, like flakes of putrid snow, on my rations. I blew off the ashes, waved at the flies, and dug in.

I was halfway through dinner when Touchberry and Wolfman, our mascot, a mongrel puppy, joined me. The puppy had something in his mouth. He dropped it at my feet. I looked at it once and then looked away. He pawed it, played with it, and then he ate it. Touchberry scratched the pup's ears.

"What did you have there, boy?"

The pup licked Touchberry's fingers.

"What was that he had?" he asked me.

I told him.

"A human hand."

From then on, we never knew, when Wolfman licked our hands—"Get lost, you little cannibal!"—what his motives were.

I had written my mother about our mascot and she had mailed me a package. Handley delivered it personally—"People Crackers for Dogs."

"Our mascot just ate a human hand," I told him.

"I've never had so many volunteers for convoy duty," Handley said. "The thrill of the open road."

One of Handley's drivers sidled up to me and asked, "Hey, sir, don't you need another rifle on the bunker line?"

"Our mascot just ate a human hand," I said.

"It's too scary back in town," he said.

The grunts even preferred pulling security along the highway to risking the snipers in town. On the highway, at least, they could drink a Coke and consort with the prostitutes; they weren't supposed to consort, they were just supposed to stop them, check them, and send them on their way, and they had been warned again and again that some of the girls were probably VC, but the Cokes were fifty cents and cold and the girls were girls.

The convoy departed and a chopper from Brigade arrived; out stepped a huge, black lieutenant colonel, Colonel Bradley. He introduced himself as our new Battalion commander.

"I don't anticipate any changes. Let's just take care of business."

Within a week he had been rechristened "The Bear"—the only CO we had who earned a nickname. The Bear was in a tough spot; he didn't know us, he had never commanded a battalion before, or any unit in combat, and he was fresh from a Brigade staff which was running around in circles, shrieking, "The sky is falling! The sky is falling!"

Brigade yanked half our Battalion back to protect themselves and issued detailed instructions on how the Bear was to deploy the rest of us: One company was lifted into the boonies on permanent ambush, the other was ordered to march in circles around Damron all day . . . and stand guard all night.

"Sir," Captain Rubino said, "we're just using up shoe leather out there. We can't patrol all day and stay alert all night and, what the hell—let them come to us and get killed here."

"We have to clear the area."

"Sure, but that's a walk around the block, one hour, maybe two, no sweat."

The Bear recognized good sense when he heard it and he took Captain Rubino's advice. The night was the time to be wary. As much as I could, I slept during the day and stayed up at night, and I wore my boots to bed, which is not so great for the feet—fungus grows between the toes—but when you wake up, you can grab your rifle and satchel and go.

"We had this doofus lieutenant," a sergeant said, "and I woke him up and yelled, 'they've broken through, come on,' and he said he had to put his boots on. We found him later, bent over them, a bullet in the back of his head."

We were edgy. When our mascot rolled over, stood up, and trotted into the bunker, the doc and I followed. We believed that the dog could hear enemy mortars fired farther away than we could and we believed he understood what the sound meant—woof woof: Bad stuff! The medics followed us, and when the red legs, right next door, saw us hitting the bunkers, they moved to theirs, and their neighbors ran, and theirs, until the whole fire support base was sealed tight. The pup lapped up some water from his water dish and ambled back outside.

"All right," Doc Shields said, "the water dish goes."

Etiquette according to Emily Army Post: Warn your companions of sudden moves—"Hey, guys, I'm going to get up now and go into the bunker, but I'm just getting something to read."

Roger.

We were on edge twenty-four hours a day. Some of us had bad dreams. I dreamt that I was in my car a couple of miles from home—FROM HOME!—and a soldier says, "Be careful, sir, there are gooks on the way." Some of us had trouble sleeping. The slightest unfamiliar noise would wake me. What, I wondered, would happen if a friendly came into my bunker while I was dreaming of an NVA attack?

Some of us couldn't sleep at all. Whenever the battery commander began to drift off, he would hear a voice say, *they're coming*, and he would start awake and run outside. Or he might remember instructions he should have given, instructions which he would find he had given. Or he might suddenly know "they" were massing in the tree line and he would get up, hook up a gun to a jeep, and try a round of suppressing fire.

Suppressing fire was crucial, because once the attack was launched, well, the NVA had reached the bunkers and shot at the battery commander with AKs and RPGs and an RPD and mortars, and he had had to stand in the open, exposed, take it, so now, all night long, he drove around the perimeter with a gun in tow and a caisson full of flachette rounds and he fired where the voice inside told him to fire.

The inner voice gave him good advice, too, because when he fired a round at the trees, the trees screamed back. Alert! A flare popped, machine guns fired. The redleg captain loosed another round, flachettes point blank. I heard claymores explode. Our guns fired rapidly into the tree line and sealed off the battlefield; all the NVA between the trees and the wire were trapped. If they tried to withdraw, they would have to pass through the artillery. If they came on, they would have to come through flachettes, grenades, and small arms. If they stayed where they were, they would die where they were. Every explosion echoed with screams.

In the morning we swept the wire. All we expected we'd have to do was police the bodies, but you never know, human beings are hard to kill, someone might have survived, badly wounded, hanging on only to take us with him, so the sweep was keyed up to shoot. Then we saw bodies. Adrenalin high. A body seemed to move and a grunt gave it a magazine, full-auto, eighteen rounds.

"That sucker ain't gonna dance no more."

But we wanted prisoners.

"Why'd you shoot that man?"

"Cuz it's fun."

Well, maybe he hadn't been alive. Maybe none of them were. How could they be, after everything we had thrown at them? We stood around like sightseers, looking at the grotesquely torn bodies and admiring our work, when one of the bodies jumped to its feet and ran for it. NVA. A G.I. grabbed his arm. The NVA struggled.

"Get out of the way. Let me get a shot at him."

No one could shoot. We were too close together (which saved his life). A sergeant punched him on the jaw and knocked him down, but he bounced back up. The sergeant grabbed him; the NVA almost broke free, which would have given us a clear shot, but then a private hit him in the back of the head with a shovel and he went down to stay.

"Gutsy little guy," the private said.

We wired his hands and feet together, carried him into Damron on a stretcher, and posted a guard. A Kit Carson asked the prisoner some questions. Stubborn still, he refused to answer. The scout consoled him with a drink of water. The guard was not pleased with this display of camaraderie.

"Get that little gook outta here or I'll blow him away."

Dai, our senior interpreter, decided to try his luck.

"No talk, VC?"

"What's this one going to do, kiss 'im?"

Dai put his .45 between the prisoner's eyes, cocked the hammer, and asked a question. The prisoner answered. Dai looked at us and laughed. So much for heroics.

"Now that's my kind of gook," the guard said.

PART VII

The Mayor of Ben Trahn

(1–14 March 1969)

Hi, Gene!

Got a maid inside your hootch
Who plays the hootch-maid hootchy-kootch?
Hey, Mac, that ain't Hi, Gene!

It's just to learn her tongue, you say.
"Same-same butterfly, lie day."
Hey, Mac, that ain't Hi, Gene!

She wipes her fingers on her nose
And jacks your dog off with her toes?
Hey, Mac, that ain't Hi, Gene!

Did you have to go back door
Because the front's a running sore?
Hey, Mac, that ain't Hi, Gene!

Scrub your hide and scrub your clothes,
Everywhere the fungus grows.
Hey, Mac, that ain't Hi, Gene!

Was it pink, what now is green,
Even though you clean and clean?
Hey, Mac, that ain't Hi, Gene!

Chapter 19

ARVNS, KIT CARSONS, AND MURDER

The Bear did not believe that the RVN officials were an asset and so he ordered Lt. Logan to take charge of the construction of their own fort. Lt. Logan was an "A" Company platoon leader, a direct commission on his second tour, and he was a souvenir collector.

"Do you want to see my latest? I took it off an NVA. My platoon didn't want me to, but it wasn't doing him any good, and why not? We passed him every day and I kept looking at it and the body began to stink and some of the troops objected to walking by it, but then the buzzards found him and after them the ants picked the bones pretty well, so I out with the old entrenching tool and chop the neck in two. I had to shake off the last few bits of flesh and hair and skin. See! Here's the hole my bullet made. My wife will love this."

> There's just nothing like a skull,
> Be it shiny, be it dull.
> Empty eyes, embarrassed grin.
> "Look what I'm no longer in!"

Lt. Logan was also a dog hater. One night on an ambush with scout dog and handler (at a time when we still thought scout dogs could do us some good) Lt. Logan decided to wiggle into a more comfortable position. The dog put a paw on him and bared his fangs. The handler was sound asleep.

In Damron I happened to be the audience for a short play in two acts.

Scene: Outside scout dog's bunker. G.I. stops.
ACT I.
G.I.: Can I pet your dog?
HANDLER (scratching dog's ear): Better not, he's a biter.

ACT II.
(Some time has elapsed.) Enter Lt. Logan. He walks by hootch, sees dog, dog wags tail, wriggles body, and salivates. Lt. Logan, assessing the situation, does not deviate from his path—dog lunges and nails Lt. Logan in the pants. Handler rushes out to comfort dog.

Lt. Logan was a dog handler hater, but he was also a guy who could say, "The word gook means 'ignorant foreigner,' so who are really the gooks over here?"

Lt. Logan supervised the construction of the fort. G.I.'s did most of the work, and since they knew they would have to live in what they had built, they built it solid; Lt. Logan also hired some locals—as public relations—to lay the bricks to build the house that Jack Arvn would live in. The NVA were not invited to the house-warming, but they participated anyway—to the bricks they added mortars—so the bunkers went up fast, the house more slowly.

Mess was served at the fort and overseen by a crusty old sergeant who had two stars on his CIB (Combat Infantryman's Badge), three awards for three wars: WW2, WW2.1, WW2.2.*

The sergeant loathed the lackadaisical attitude of the "hippie G.I.'s," as he called them; all his experience cried out when he saw them bunched together in the chow line.

"Spread out! Spread out! One round could get you all."

They laughed. Training slogans. Then there was a whistle, a bang, and whining fragments. On the dive to the bunker, the sergeant yelled, "Just like that one!"

When the skies were clear of mortars, the chiefs would sit in the shade of a bunker and contemplate how wealthy they would be if they were free to milk the village as they pleased, or sell us dope, but even so they were by no means the worst cog in the RVN apparatus. They were not, after all, Arvn spooks.

"We di village," the Arvn spook said.

We went to the village. The baddest boy on the Arvn's blacklist was a

---

* The army has planned for seven wars: CIB alone, CIB with a single silver star, two silver stars, three (for four wars), a single gold star (five wars), two gold stars, three gold stars (for seven wars).

man identified as the commie district chief. We discussed his where-abouts with his wife.

"Your husband around?"

"He's at the fort," she said, "laying bricks. Shall I get him?"

"Yes, please, if you would."

She got him.

VC District Chief? He looked to me like what he said he was, a hum-ble peasant bricklayer. And, furthermore, if I'd been a VC District Chief and I had heard that an Arvn spook was asking for me, I'd have fled to the hills, whereas he looked as calm and unworried as a simple peasant bricklayer should be. His expression changed, of course, when the Arvn psyops chung-wi hit him in the face with his swagger stick and knocked him down.

The chung-wi kicked him in the ribs, ground a cigarette out on his neck, and hit him again with the swagger stick, but he couldn't shake the role of simple peasant bricklayer (torn into for reasons beyond his com-prehension), and he couldn't beat a confession out of him, even though he kicked him again and again and shouted questions at him. Names of the infrastructure. Locations. Intentions.

Well, the joke was on us. Our suspect *was* a simple peasant bricklayer; the informant who had put him on the blacklist was paying off a personal grudge. The Arvn shrugged. Win some, lose some.

We hated the Arvns.

We had planned to start a school, to teach the children to read and write, and also to sing the Vietnamese national anthem, but the school supplies had disappeared among the Arvns. Only now that we had se-cured this area, did they dare come . . . to roust the villagers and drive them back into the arms of the VC.

The villagers did not hate us. We played with their children and we held a medcap every day; we treated their minor ailments (with aspirin, penicillin, and soap) and we diagnosed the major ailments and advised them to go to the hospital, and we never requisitioned food or labor. And yet we knew that our actions were irrelevant—we had no chance in this war, in this hamlet—unless we kept the Arvns out.

One of the village boys named Grip was learning to speak English. He was the oldest boy in the hamlet, about fourteen years old, and soon he would have to make up his mind about becoming an Arvn or a VC. In the meantime I cultivated him. One day after a medcap in Ben Tranh I asked him, "Are there any tunnels nearby?"

"Uhnh," he said (i.e., yeah) and showed me one.

"Son of a gun," I muttered.

The entrance was too narrow for my shoulders. Redd and Kirksey were also too large; Dai and Tien had assessed the situation and quietly departed. Curiosity, however, had drawn Mighty Mouse and another Kit Carson scout to the tunnel.

"Well, Mouse," I said, "I give you my .45."

"No, captain," he said.

"Yes, Mouse," I said.

Sweat popped out on his forehead. What if the tunnel was booby-trapped? What if we had cornered a wild VC? He studied my face and there read a grim future if he refused, so he took the .45 and disappeared down the hole. I tried to look in all directions at once—would a VC pop out of the earth? Would there be an ominous rumble below, as of, say, a discharged AK? And, if there was, what then? But Mouse popped up . . . in a suspiciously short time. The tunnel, he explained, was only twenty meters in length. He described it to the other scout and the other scout nodded and explained it to us. He pointed at the entrance.

"VC here. VC shoot. Di-di. Di-di here."

He pointed at the exit.

"Ah," Redd said, "he means that the VC would pop up, shoot at us, and then crawl through the tunnel, and escape out the back."

The scout nodded. He had been VC not so long ago and he kind of forgot whose side he was on now.

"VC shoot. Di-di. Numba one."

"Number one?"

"Uh, no, numba ten, VC numba ten."

The Engineers I summoned were enthusiastic.

"Haven't had a chance to blow a tunnel in weeks," the sergeant in charge said. "Are you sure the tunnel's clear?"

Of course I wasn't. Maybe the Mouse had ducked down, taken one sniff, smelled human occupants, and popped right back out again.

"Sure," I said.

He whistled as he went below with his det cord, fuses, and C-4. After a short time he reappeared and led wires out to a detonator.

"I've been blowing holes for bunkers," he said. "Boring."

He attached the wires to the detonator.

"What I like," he said, "is something constructive like this, blowing a tunnel. Everybody likes it. Just look at the people."

The villagers had gathered to watch.

"Sidewalk superintendents."

Yes, but as none of them spoke English and none of us spoke Vietnamese, I wondered how we were going to explain to them that we were blowing the tunnel and they should vacate the area.

I waved my hands.

They waved back.

I pointed.

They smiled.

I said, "Boom!"

They said, "Boom!"

"Let me have a go, sir," the Engineer sergeant said.

He faced the crowd.

"Fire in the hole!"

They screamed and ran.

"I've done this before," he said.

At the evening meeting I reported on the incident—Lessons Learned: Make Friends In The Village. (I did wonder if the boy would be alive in the morning.) I emphasized how helpful the scouts had been. They were loyal to us, not to the Arvns, and they did what we said. Later, when I said a few good words about them to an Arvn interpreter, he shrugged.

"When the war is over, we kill this trash."

Mouse worked for "C" Company.

"Mouse is a tiger," Captain Ervin said. "A few more like him and we just might get out of this fracas. Once we were in this village, Mouse was walking beside me, and I was watching the point, when all of a sudden this gook with a pistol in his hand steps out of a hootch. I was just thinking, I've had it, when the Mouse cuts loose with a whole mag. He hates gooks worse than we do."

Captain Ervin gave Mouse the pistol as a reward.

When they returned to Damron an Arvn interpreter—the only one then in camp—asked if he could look at the pistol. Mouse let him. The Arvn walked off with it. The Mouse went and got his rifle. The Arvn fled to TOC for protection. (I was in town.) The Mouse went after him.

"Two gooks with guns," the Bear told me, "and me in the middle and no one knew what the hell they were jabbering about. I thought they were going to shoot it out right there."

The Bear separated them. The Arvn hopped on the convoy back to town. The Mouse rode in with a Coke girl—sure death if the NVA had been watching the road. The Arvn went to the medics' hootch, the interpreters' home away from home. (The medics wanted them to find another, because the Arvns liked to have a couple of beers and then shoot their rifles off through the ceiling; a medic finally got fed up and told them the next time they shot their rifles off he was going to clean their clocks). The Mouse followed the Arvn to the hootch, stood at the door, and yelled for him to come outside. The Arvn appeared in the doorway and Mouse shot him, once in the chest and once in the head.

When I arrived the Mouse was standing by himself. He wasn't mad anymore, just bewildered. Why had he done it?

"God!" the medic told me. "I thought the gooks were doing it again and so I ran outside and I see this Arvn folding to the ground and I say, uh-oh, and I grab the scout and he doesn't resist and so I've got him. What's it all about?"

I made formal identification of the Arvn (though the first bullet had crushed the side of his head and made him almost unrecognizable); the other bullet had struck his shoulder, tumbled through the body and exited above the knee. A crowd gathered. An American voyeur in the crowd stretched out his hand toward the pistol.

No way, G.I.

I escorted murderer and pistol to Arvn headquarters.

Two G.I.'s from "C" Company showed up.

"What are the gooks going to do with him?"

"I guess they'll try him and then they'll shoot him."

"Can't we get him back? He's a good guy."

"He did kill an Arvn."

"Yeah, well . . ."

Not like it was a human being.

Chapter 20

WHERE'S THE BATHROOM?

On the evening of 7 March I was sitting with the surgeon outside the aid station, and we were both wishing we had a martini, wishing the nights were shorter, wishing the moon were full, thinking about our cots . . . and how much we hated abrupt awakenings . . . and how much I wanted to see the night through, but I was sleepy, it was late, and I stood up to go to my bunker.

A bullet cracked past my head.

I sat down. A firefight broke out at the bunker line. I slid down the steps leading to the aid station bunker. A medic crouched next to me.

"Well, sports fans," he said, "here we are at the Boonie U Arena and it's a great evening for this renewal of the Army-NVA duel. Both sides appear ready and I think I can safely say we're going to have some real fireworks."

". . . I'm Dufus McCrae and here with me tonight is someone all you Army fans will remember—Joe Bisatz. How do the two sides look to you, Joe?"

"Well, Doof, let's face it. NVA doesn't have the size of Army, but they're gutsy little guys with an excellent ground attack and they don't know when they're licked. They just keep coming till they wear you down."

"I've heard the rap on them is that they don't seem to have the old zip anymore."

"Yeah, Doof, you can't deny they've lost men they can't replace and injuries will play a part."

"What about their plan of attack? Some say it's unimaginative."

"We've seen them quite a few times this year and, sure, they use the same old weapons on offense, but, as we say in the business, don't worry how you got there, just keep on pushing."

'Okay, folks, you've just heard Joe Bisatz, the man who wrote the book on NVA, and along with him tonight—and glad to be here—I'm Dufus McCrae. Now what about Army, Joe."

"Doof, Army has a great defense and an explosive aerial attack. They can kill you from anywhere on the field."

"I've heard they have some morale problems, though, Joe."

"Reporters, Doof. Reporters always talk about the locker room when nothing's happening on the field. Sure, Army's had a big turnover in personnel and they lack something in consistency, but let me tell you one thing, it's different down there in the trenches than it is up here, and from where I sit, I say they'll find it when they need it. I expect a real ding-dong battle."

A squad of NVA was caught in the wire. The spook lieutenant (S-2) suggested to the Bear that a patrol go out and collect a prisoner.

"Good thinking," the Bear said. "I'll get you a platoon."

"Urg," the spook said, but he had no choice and he wasn't a wimp anyway, so, when the platoon was mustered, he told them, "We're going to get as close as we can and then call for illumination."

(With three clicks on the handset.)

He grabbed the point man by the belt and said, "Our mission is to take a prisoner, so, please, don't shoot unless you have to."

He walked directly behind him.

We got up next to the wire. Our guys are pros—I was right there with them and I still couldn't hear them make a sound.

He gave the signal on the handset. The area was illuminated.

In the light of the flares I saw three NVA in the wire . . . and the three NVA saw us.

One NVA swung his AK up with his finger on the trigger. The point shot him and killed him.

I couldn't argue with that.

Another reached for the AK he had dropped on the ground. The point shot him once and the enemy lay still. The third man's AK was caught in the wire. He struggled to free it. The point aimed his M-16.

Oh no, I thought, go through all this and not get a prisoner? I tugged on the point's belt.

"Please don't shoot him. Please don't shoot him."

He touched the NVA's face with the muzzle . . . and the NVA surrendered. We cut him loose and took him to TOC for interrogation. (Only one interpreter had not been granted leave for Tet; he was on duty at TOC.)

The wounded NVA—he had a bullet through the upper chest—was

carried to the aid station. The surgeon patched him up; I gave him a cigarette; a crowd of adrenalin-high voyeurs gathered around him. One of the medics consulted a Vietnamese phrase book and asked him a question. The prisoner shook his head—he didn't understand—and held out his hand for the book. The medic showed it to him.

Where is the bathroom?

The medic laughed. The prisoner didn't seem to have a sense of humor, but he did look alert and intelligent, so I took the book and tried a different question:

What rank are you?

"Tiwi."

"Tiwi?"

He nodded. I called TOC.

"Are you getting anything from your prisoner?"

"Naw. He's dumb as a stump."

"Well, the wounded man here is a second lieutenant."

The spook hurried over and the tiwi spilled his guts. (No one had ever told him not to.) He had been the commander of a sapper platoon. The platoon was supposed to cut a lane through the wire for the assault force, which would assemble at the plantation house and move forward—if all went as planned—at midnight. We checked our watches. 2350.

Right.

Where is your base camp?

The tiwi marked the position of his base camp on our maps.

Fire mission!

The first rounds were on their way when the Brigade chopper arrived to fetch the tiwi back for staff playtime.

"Those little buggers are hard to figure," Touchberry said. "They live like rats. They starve. We sling napalm and HE and willy-peter at them."

"Not to mention the Big Hurt in the sky," Redd said.

"Yeah, and they attack us, fifty or a hundred of them against a prepared position. And for what?"

"Gangrene," Redd said. "Malaria, dengue fever, typhus, typhoid, tetanus."

"They must think they're going to win."

The Bear sat me down with a cup of coffee to shoot some philosophy.

"You've studied history. Tell me, why are we always on the wrong side?"

"Great powers are always on the wrong side. We get the quislings, they have the patriots."

"So how do you see things here?"

"It reminds me," I said, "of the war between Athens and Sparta."

"In that case," the Bear said, "I better have a refill on that coffee."

"The Spartans planned to march to the gates of Athens, the Athenian army would come out, they would fight a battle, the Athenians would lose, and the Spartans would dictate terms. The Athenians planned to harass the coasts of Sparta with their fleet until the Spartans agreed to Athenian terms."

"If I remember rightly, neither strategy worked."

"The Athenians refused to come out and fight a battle and the Spartans endured the harassment of their coasts."

"The point being . . . ?"

"Both sides based their strategy on a misconception."

"And so do we, you say. What's our misconception?"

"Well, sir, even assuming we break the NVA, what are we offering these people?"

Division said that we were offering "to protect a terrorized young government as it seeks the basic human freedoms for its people."

The Bear put it better.

"Saigon."

We knew that the NVA were well-trained and highly motivated and we had a high opinion of them, but they lived under relentless pressure, and by 1969 their morale was beginning to crack. They had no code of conduct (the tiwi we captured seemed to have no qualms about fingering his comrades) and the Hoi Chanh program (welcome home, VC) was working—VC, and a few NVA, came over to us and fought against their former comrades. One NVA lieutenant led American patrols. An NVA medic worked for me.

For several nights we fired interdicting missions at the locations the prisoner had given us. On the third morning I received a call.

"Come to the gate."

"What's up?"

"There's a mob of villagers here."

They were clustered around a red-eyed, crazed-looking woman and a rolled-up blanket. One sniff told me the story. Burned flesh. The villagers unrolled the blanket and, sure enough, there were three little children, charred so black they flaked. When the woman saw the bodies, she screamed, threw herself on Redd, and sank her teeth into his side. The villagers grabbed her and tried to pull her off as Redd went for his .45.

"I was going to blow her away," he said, "but then I've got children myself and I just figured how I'd feel."

The mother had left her children alone and spent the night with "relatives." When she returned home in the morning, she found the bodies in the ashes of her hootch and she brought them to the fire support base to accuse us.

Someone had blundered.

We hoped we could prove the blunderers were NVA, that they had shot a rocket at us—I thought the hut was in the village—and missed, so the FO, myself, Redd, and a new medic nicknamed Alphabet (because of the intricacy of his name) started out to investigate. Madam Fred stopped me.

"Where you go?"

"With her," I said, suddenly losing all confidence in the proposition.

"No, captain, no. Bad place. Cross river. Beaucoup VC."

I returned to the FSB—it's not hard to distrust a woman whose children you've burned to a crisp—and I requested a few troops. (Once I had collected some troops, the prostitutes felt safe enough to tag along.) We had to cross a stream and follow a narrow path, perfect for an ambush, before we saw the burned-out hut in a little clearing. We examined the ground. The evidence was clear. Our artillery had fallen, the children had run to the bunker inside the hootch, the hootch caught fire, the children suffocated and then they were incinerated. The FO wanted me to explain to the mother that the Arvns were to blame, not the U.S. Artillery.

"Tell her, Arvns mark map, here be no hootches, VC, all VC. Their mistake, not American."

Nonetheless—Good News!—we would pay compensation.

"Sorry, mama, here's 150 pi. Go drop another litter."

And we promised to build her a new hootch, so everything was jake.

The next day a boy in the village had his leg blown off by a mine which the VC had set in the rice paddies.

"I should have gone to Canada," Redd said.

"And the NVA should have gone to China."

But they hadn't and we hadn't, so we did our job and tried not to think about it too much and mostly ignored the news from The World. College students didn't want to be drafted, go to war, maybe lose an arm, or leg, or head. Who did?

Di Canada.

"Don't you think that'd be worse, an exile, away from your family and friends?"

"There ain't nothing worse."

"The Canadians treat 'em like heroes."

"Mutual ass-grabbers."

"Still, they can't come home."

"It beats going home in a bag, don't it?"

"Damn straight it do."

"They should have stayed in college."

"College!"

"Me, I got nothing against students. The way I figure, they're just doing what we want to do, drink beer, smoke dope, trap beaver."

"Yeah . . . and riot."

"What really gets my case is the National Guard."

"That route-step bunch of bastards."

"They should ship their asses over here."

"That'd help charlie."

"They're as bad as the draft dodgers."

"As bad? Who joins the guard except draft dodgers?"

"Football players."

"I rest my case."

"Hell, I'd even join the guard, it got me out of here, cuz, cousin, there ain't nothing worse than right here, right now. Like they used to say, I'm going straight to heaven, cuz I done my time in hell."

By and large, we believed in live and let live, but we did make some exceptions. Jean Paul Sartre, who opposed the U.S. involvement in Vietnam, had noticed he couldn't say gauche without spraying a dozen liberal zealots, aflame with the fire of a righteous cause, and so he decided to form a brigade, the Jean-Paul-Sartre Brigade, which would come to Nam and fight beside their brothers, the NVA, or rather, that is, the VC, I mean, the NLF.

"I'd re-up for six, if I could get a crack at that."

We blamed the French. Why not? We were risking our lives to clean up their mess. Or, if we weren't, then what were we fighting for? Apple pie? Election day speeches? To turn a buck for the military-industrial complex? . . . which had fouled up all the way from the twenty-round clip that couldn't hold twenty rounds to the Tropic Bar.

What was the answer?

Chapter 21

COLD FEET

Colonel Bradley had lots of good ideas—more aggressive activity in the hamlets, a stand-down and training exercise, the emphasis on performance against appearance—and he had one bad idea: The Contest.

The victorious platoon would win a free weekend at beautiful Vung Tau, all expenses paid—no entry fee, no purchase required, anyone can win.

The Rules

1. For every bag of VC rice captured, add five points.
2. For every VC weapon or 100 rounds of VC ammunition, add ten points. (Unexpended ammunition only.)
3. For every VC body, add fifty points.
4. For every VC prisoner, including hoi chanhs, add 100 points.
5. For every U.S. whiskey, deduct fifty points.
6. For every U.S. kilo, deduct 100 points.
   Highest Score Wins!

As Touchberry pointed out, there was a loophole in the rules on deductions.

"Since no points are deducted for guys missing in action, why don't we just leave the kilos out there?"

I could see that this might start a whole new trend in reporting casualties to the next of kin. Instead of the usual letter of condolence:

Dear Mrs. Brown:
Remember your son Fred?

Tough luck! He's dead.
            Department of the Army.

Or telegram:
    DEPARTMENT OF THE ARMY TO MRS. BRAGG:
    YOUR SON'S COMING HOME IN A BAG.

We might have:

    D. A. TO MRS. JANEY JOYNTS:
    YOU MUST DEDUCT A HUNDRED POINTS.

Before we knew it, letters had been sent to the world—"putting a point value on human life"—and a reporter from *Time* appeared. A story was printed, and, as usual, the media got it all wrong. Our objection was not some wimp-out on assigning a point value to human life but on assigning a point value to American lives—a grunt, the argument went, didn't let himself get killed on purpose, so it is unfair to deduct points for kilos.

In fact, the contest made us more humane. You got more points for live prisoners than for body count, and, as delicate as that moment is, when the enemy decide they've had enough and they want to come over: "Chieu hoi! Chieu hoi!" they call—a phrase intelligible to both sides— and they hesitantly stand up and walk toward us. Then each G.I. must make his own decision. Has the would-be hoi chanh carried on the firefight all night long, when he was trapped but still had hopes of escape, and has he, now in the light of day, knowing the situation to be hopeless, called out, "Chieu hoi?"

"Chieu hoi," he calls and comes forward, hands in the air.

"No way, sucker," a G.I. says . . . and blows him away.

Only a wimp could object to that, except now, with the contest, the platoon leader could say, "Dammit, you just cost us fifty points."

(Lt. Logan's platoon won the contest. They were enthusiastic about their vacation trip to the fleshpots of Vung Tau, until their plane became airborne and the landing gear fell off.)

The Contest was not one of Colonel Bradley's better ideas. His best idea was the stand-down and training exercise. For three days the Battalion read maps, sighted their rifles, practiced marksmanship, maneuvered, checked equipment, and discussed operations. One afternoon the officers got together in Dau Tieng and talked about strengths and weaknesses.

"Don't send us out for three days and then tell us, once we're out there, that we got to stay a week," Lt. Yates said.

He had already told that to the Brigade commander. He had been fetched in, to report, and, in his week-old fatigues and week-old whiskers, he had chewed out the Brigade CO.

"When you tell us three days and you leave us out there a week, you're just telling us, you've got your head up your ass. That scares us."

The staff officers were aghast, but the Brigade commander had grown tired of staff boot-lickers, and soon Lt. Yates found himself appointed aide to the CO.

Captain Wong (now "B" Company commander) said, "We went out for three days and three nights. The first day, we were raring to get at the enemy. The first night we wanted him to enter our ambush. We wanted contact. The next day and the next night we were beginning to wear down and the third day and the third night we were tired and we were scared."

The S-3 summed it up.

"So what you're saying is, go in on day one, come out on day three, hit and run."

"Unless we make heavy contact," the Bear said.

"We just want to know," Lt. Yates said, "that you know what you're doing and not tell us what we have to do and then change your mind once we're out there."

We left unsaid the greatest lesson—Brigade staff did not know how to run an operation. Inevitably, staff officers who have not been on line, and most of them had not been, do not appreciate the practical limits of human endurance—to them we were colored pins on a board. Battalions must (in self-defense) originate their own operations.

What we needed from Brigade, Division, and MAC-V was a scheme to force the NVA to come out and fight. They never could figure out how to do that.

The meeting also tried to analyze how we compared with the NVA.

"When I'm out there," a platoon leader said, "I feel like I'm a stranger in territory they know like the back of their hand. I feel like the enemy knows where we are, how many we are, and what we're going to do. And I get tired fast."

"I think," I said, "that maybe we're overstating how much at home the NVA are. Sure, they speak the language, but they aren't welcome in the South. The Southern villagers believe that the Northerners are here to conquer them."

We also believed that the NVA were better in the boonies than we were. Sure, we had all the material advantages—B-52s, artillery, and tactical airpower, adequate food and good medical care—but "Americans are not at home in the jungle."

A MAC-V adviser had told me, "You can't beat the NVA in stealth. They can sneak up on you and cut your throat before you know it."

To which I replied, "Bull."

The NVA feared us, not only because of our material advantage, but because we had the edge in small unit tactics.

"We're so quiet out there," Lt. Roe told me, "that sometimes it can scare you at night. You think your men have all taken off."

When our men were on night ambush, they didn't smoke, eat, or drink.

"What about calls of nature?" I asked Lt. Roe.

"If I have to take a leak, I just go in my pants," he said.

In the whole time we were around Dau Tieng, putting out ambushes every day, the NVA never once spotted an ambush. One time, when a platoon was ambushing a trail during the day . . .

"We weren't really expecting anything," the machine gunner told me. "We were just lying low and the next thing I knew, there were the NVA. They just popped out of the brush right in among us. And that NVA point knew something was wrong. He stopped and he looked around, and wherever he looked, he pointed his AK. He was standing right over the M-60, one foot on each side of it.

"I was puckered to a pinhead then, I'll tell you, but he never looked down.

"God!

"As soon as he lifted his leg, I yanked that gun up and let him have it."

"Think," Captain Wong said, "how scared they must be. We could be anywhere anytime in any force. They're more scared than we are. After all, they come over to us, we don't go over to them."

We continued to receive a steady trickle of VC and NVA hoi chanhs.

Our problem was twofold: First, finding the enemy—he was less and less willing to come out and fight us—and, second, marksmanship (which was one of the reasons for the training stand-down).

Lt. Logan was out on daylight ambush when two VC on bicycles entered the killzone. He stood up. They froze and then they raised their hands. He, and his command group, approached them. Lt. Logan lifted their rifles. Then one of the VC shoved Lt. Logan and both jumped on their bikes and pedalled down the length of the killzone. They got away.

Colonel Bradley said, "What you've got to do is wait until they're so close you can shoot them and then just reach out and take the wallet out of their hip pocket."

We also had the problem of health and hygiene.

Every officer is charged with the duty of overseeing the physical and mental well-being of his men—for instance, malaria tablets. Troops do not like the large orange tablet (or the little white ones either), so an officer must stand in the mess line every Monday and hand each troop the orange tablet and watch him swallow it and check his name off a roster. (An officer could be court-martialled for an outbreak of malaria in his unit.)

Officers are also supposed to exercise command responsibility in the never-ending battle against VD.

"I am tired of the clap," the Bear said. "If I could, I'd run a whore-house myself, and make sure the girls were clean, but someone would ask, what was your rake-off, so I can't, but I am tired of men not being in the field because they have the clap."

"We could," the Battalion surgeon suggested, "take the shots to them on the resupply choppers, and the medics could give them the shots out there."

Ever since the surgeon had let the cat out of the bag about that little island off Japan, we could no longer pretend that the consequences might be permanent quarantine, nor were the officers exactly leading by example. It was well known—and possibly even true—that Lt. Eugene Maclecher (as we called him) was the father of his hootchmaid's little baby-san, and not only that, but he was also well on his way to becoming father-designate for the second time with the same hootchmaid . . . in one tour.

"Geez, didn't you even wait for the bag to drop?" Bobby L asked him.

Gene suggested that I, as a captain, should order his fellow lieutenants to stop spreading these vicious rumors; his strenuous efforts to scotch the gossip had its effect: We all became convinced that the gossip was true. He was even made the subject of a song, *Hi, Gene*. Anyway, we quit our efforts to stamp out fornication and we limited ourselves to diagnosis and treatment of the symptoms.

We also had to conduct regular foot-and-head (I mean, the large lump atop the neck) inspections—troops must not allow themselves to become a culture medium for the bugs and bacilli of the teeming Orient. (I had tried a mustache myself, before I learned my lesson—one day I ran a finger across the mustache and a good-sized clump of hair fell out . . . connected to a good-sized chunk of my face.)

In short, officers must ensure that their soldiers remain functional members of the unit until their tour is up or they stop metal. Americans have trouble with authority. The kids on line, and those who had been on line, respected only the line—*I'll take orders from the guy whose butt is hanging out with mine and no one else*—and they were suspicious of the

SFCs, the triple rockers, the sergeant major, staff officers, the Brass, in a word, Lifers.

The Lifers thought respect should come with the territory and that the kids had an attitude problem. The Lifers didn't like the slogans: *Kill a commie for Christ* or *I'll be home for Christmas in a Christmas box.* They hated the songs. "Don't give a damn 'bout that Vietnam."

The sergeant major heard a song that Redd was singing ("Bang, bang, your son is dead") and ordered him to stop ASAP, and then the sergeant major saw me.

"You shouldn't let that soldier sing songs like that," he said.

General Order Number Sixty-Nine: It has come to the attention of headquarters that personnel of this command are expressing complaints. Complaints will cease forthwith.

(Signed) F.T.A. Two Stars, Commanding General

I touched my captain's bars and said, "I like the songs."

The SM ran to the Bear. He wanted Redd back on line. The Bear invited me to a private conversation.

Now the Bear had once said to the private who brought the morning coffee, "Take that back to the cook and tell him it's so bad I wouldn't even want him to drink it."

And the cook had spent a day and a night in the field to meditate on his responsibility to the culinary arts.

"The sergeant major," the Bear said to me, "isn't pleased with these protest songs."

"I know, sir."

"He's our senior NCO. We have to support our NCOs."

"Yes sir."

"What about this soldier singing them?"

"He's a medic, sir. He's an asset to civic action."

"All right. I've had my say. We'll leave it at that for now."

I tried to clue the sergeant major in on kids and protest songs, but he thought that griping was detrimental to discipline and good order. He didn't even like the harmless verse published by the yard in our Battalion paper. Mostly the poetry took advantage of rhymed couplets like friend/end, death/breath, why/die, mud/blood, right/fight, said/dead. For instance,

I have a friend
Who met his end,
But ere his death
This final breath,
"I wonder why

That I must die
In blood-soaked mud.
Can this be right,
That men should fight?"
And thus he said
And then was dead.

To which I thought of this reply:

Roll Over, Wilfred Owen, Roll.

Dulce et decorum est
That you are at your final rest.
Or do such lines torment the soul?
Roll over, Wilfred Owen, Roll.

Are there angels up in space
Weeping for the human race
Because of all our "don't know why
But some must fight and some must die?"

And die in countless measured feet
That strike a four iambic beat?
Do these verses reach to hell,
Torment the angels, those who fell? . . .

. . . reach the grave where Wilfred lies
(In the hope someday he'll rise)? . . .
. . . torment his body as his soul?
Roll over, Wilfred Owen, Roll.

After my conversation with the Bear, the operations officer asked me,
as S-5, to tell him how we could pacify the villages in our AO. I made the
mistake of telling him the truth.
"Secure them."
"We don't have the troops."
"Then we can't pacify them. You can't pacify terrorized people. They
have to know they won't be killed. It's not enough to show the flag."
"You have to convince them that freedom is worth fighting for."
"We'd have to convince them that freedom is worth being dead for."
He told the Bear that I wasn't doing my job. All in all, it was a down
time.

"Cheer up, sir," Redd said. "What the heck, I was saving a package from home. Let's open it."

Inside his package was a note from his folks:

We found these in a store. They seemed like just the thing. Hope you enjoy them.

Two dozen Tropic Bars.

And then I was called to the gate about a woman. As soon as she saw me, she dropped to her knees and began to wail.

Cheoi-oi, cheoi-oi.

Her cheeks were wet with tears. I sent someone to fetch Sunny.

What has happened?

Her son had been drafted, against his will, an Arvn. The VC came to the village during the night. They took her husband away, tortured him, and murdered him. His body lay in the reeds by the river. She had lost her boy and now her husband was killed.

Cheoi-oi, cheoi-oi.

What do you want us to do?

She was afraid to get the body. What if the VC were there? They would kill her. She needed help to carry the body. The neighbors were afraid.

Where is the body now?

By the river. She would show us.

While I thought it over, she squatted down and wailed.

Cheoi-oi, cheoi-oi.

Her grief seemed staged, like a tragic queen saying, *alas, alas, alack-a-day, oh, woe is me,* but Madam Fred vouched for her—she did live in the village and her husband was missing—so I rustled up a platoon (and Redd, Sunny, and an Argentinian photographer).

The Argentinian had come to the United States to make his fortune as a photographer. Then one day the Argentinian embassy had called him and told him that his father was dying and he needed to come over immediately. He rushed to the embassy. A member of the staff met him and told him, "You are now on Argentinian soil, you have been drafted, you have six months to report, or else."

"What about my father?"

"Oh, he's fine."

The term of enlistment in the Argentinian army was six years. He elected to remain in the United States as a resident alien . . . and he was drafted.

He went along with us to take pictures. I told the patrol, "This woman says her husband has been murdered by the VC. We are going to help her collect the body. There's a chance that the NVA have ambushed the corpse, so be alert."

I let the woman go ahead of me up the road; I walked right behind her so I could shoot her if she led us into an ambush, though I didn't tell her that—let it come as a surprise—and she ambled along like a ruminating cow and led us to a village on the banks of the river. The village was empty and silent. A hootch had burned to the ground; smoke rose from the smouldering ruins. Pots of breakfast rice gave off steam. A sow lay dead on the ground. Redd kicked the body.

> Can death be sleep
> When life is but a dream
> And visions of our former selves
> Pass as a dead pig by?

There wasn't a sound or movement except our sounds and our movements and the flowing water of the river. The platoon leader said he didn't like it. Me neither.

If I were the NVA I would spring the ambush when we picked the body up, when we would be distracted by the corpse.

The men around me waited. The S-3 came overhead in a loach and I ordered two men to fetch the body—best to do what we had to do, while we had eyes overhead.

If I were the NVA, now would be the time, now when the two men were easy targets and our eyes were on them.

I knelt. The closer to the ground the better. The chopper came around again. We were all on one knee. The two men reached the river. The chopper dipped below the forest edge.

Now.

The men brought the body to us and placed it on a stretcher.

The victim had been shot below the left eye; the wound was ringed with powder burns and half the face was black with coagulated blood. His body was bruised from the beating.

"Let's di-di," I said and I told Redd and the photographer, "Pick up the stretcher."

"I'm not going to carry him," the photographer said.

Anger at his disobedience hit me so hard, my rational mind blacked out. I yelled his name and started for him. I don't know what I was going to do to him, but before I had taken the three steps to reach him and do it, he had grabbed his end of the stretcher. The members of the patrol laughed. The stretcher bearers walked out in silence, except when Redd said, "This guy's feet are cold."

A group of villagers met us and took the body. The widow thanked us. And that was that . . . except the S-3 asked me, "Why'd you kneel down? See something?"

"No. I thought we might be ambushed. I wanted to be ready."

"Why did you expect an ambush?"

"The situation. There weren't any villagers around."

"Uh-huh. Well, we were listening to our captured radio and intercepted a conversation between a couple of Chinese advisers and one was asking the other whether he should engage you."

Gee, thanks for keeping it a secret.

Chapter 22

VILLAGE IDYLL

On a typical day I would rise before dawn (about seven), shave, have breakfast (bacon, a hunk of bread, reconstituted eggs, coffee), sit in the early morning shade (though it would be a bit cool), and discuss with my interpreters, my medics, and Kirksey, what we were going to do that day. About ten we would pick up our gear, I would set out on foot, they would follow in the truck, and we would make for a hootch not far from the fire support base. I walked, because I wanted to see whether people were up and about and children were running hither and yon, and how they reacted to me; if I felt no tension, then I knew the hootch hadn't been boobytrapped and it wasn't ambushed and we could relax and treat the people who came to us.

As we crossed the wire, we crossed a line between the First World and the Third World. We left electricity, clean water, canned food, cigarettes, literacy (books, magazines, *Stars and Stripes*), radio, TV, air-conditioning, hot coffee, and we entered a world where people still believed in witch-craft.

Pére Michelin instructed them to drink clean water and eat good food, but they obeyed only as they obeyed all authority, not because they saw any connection between sanitation and good health. Demons caused sickness. At this particular time the "plague demon" was stalking the Michelin. When we went the round of the hamlets to give plague shots, the villagers believed either that we were sticking needles in them for our own divertisement or that we were using American demons to work a counterspell to the plague demon.

They believed in sympathetic treatment.

"They're not so dumb," Speedy said. "When you have a headache, there's nothing better than a pretty girl massaging your temples."

"Temples?" said a cynic. "Is that what you call them?"

"Hey," Speedy said to me, "I'm not kidding. When I have a headache, she massages my temples and my forehead and then she pinches the bridge of my nose as hard as she can and it draws the pain to the surface and the headache is gone. It really works."

Maybe the treatment worked for minor pains, but the villagers also used it for serious illnesses, of which the pain was symptomatic. A woman in the village, who had had Lord-knows-what—goiter perhaps or tonsillitis—had been massaged and pinched and pulled and pinched again, until her throat was turned into a hideous mass of scar tissue.

Even those with some education, who knew that we had medicine to cure them, believed that the medicine had to be applied directly to the afflicted spot. One of our Kit Carson scouts with a headache taped an aspirin to his forehead.

And the villagers were so poor . . . A soldier walking through the hamlet picked up what he thought was a little pile of junk—a cooking pot and a broom. The woman who owned it complained to me that the G.I. had stolen it and I got it back for her and gave the G.I. a little lecture.

"Don't take anything."

He said, "I thought it was junk."

"I don't doubt it, but you have to understand that what looks to us like junk to them is not."

He said, "Those poor people."

They lived in their own filth. The village smelled of vegetation and sweat and human waste. Our fire support base smelled of insecticide (we could sleep without mosquito bars), burning excrement (from the five hundred or so inhabitants of the fire support base), the urine-soaked ground around the piss tubes, asphalt, cordite, and of the five hundred men themselves.

Going from the fire support base to the hamlet was also going from a plowed, unshaded, flat, noisy area, where the sun beat down on the bunkers, over to a shady, green, quiet town, where a breeze was always blowing. The people lived in harmony with their environment (they had no choice), while we tore the top off the land, before we built our base.

Sergeant Tien, my Arvn interpreter, took me on a tour of the hamlet. The people grew, or manufactured, almost everything they needed; every plant in the hamlet was functional except for a few flowers. One tree provided a cottony substance for stuffing pillows (and wounds), another provided juice to cure constipation (an ever-present threat in a rice-consuming populace), tables of various herbs provided seasonings, and vegetable gardens surrounded the hamlet.

I particularly admired the skills of one man, who had been in the

French army and was now the hamlet craftsman. He collected whatever scrap metal he could and out of it he made pots and pans. He had no solder, so he had to crimp the pots together. The lids he fashioned fit precisely on the top of the pot. We gave the children pipe cleaners and the next thing we'd know, they would have twisted them into M-16s or AKs. Once a week those individuals with something to sell or something to buy would walk to the market in Dau Tieng (a trip of two to ten miles depending on the hamlet).

The children growing up in the hamlets saw everything. They lived in a single hut with their parents and their grandparents and their brothers and sisters and, perhaps, the wives and husbands of their brothers and sisters. They followed the G.I.'s and the prostitutes into the bushes and thus acquired a practical knowledge of the functions of the parts of the body. They witnessed birth and death and violent injury.

The Vietnamese were at home in their world. They lived close to the graves of their ancestors, whom they revered. We were not supposed to be able to understand this—so wiser Western heads had said—and partly we could not, because we did not value the family as they did, but partly we could, because we had our own dead.

We didn't feel that our friends who had died had dissolved into nothingness. We felt as though they had turned a corner in a path we all were forced to take and that we would walk along behind them and turn the same corner—perhaps that very day—and see them again. We Wolfhounds interacted as though we were a family, the largest family any of us would ever know.

"Once," the old man told me, "we have a king. He is bad man—*qu'est que c'est tyrannique?*"

"A tyrant."

"Oui. A tyrant. He has an aide—a general. This general, he does not like king. He plan coup d'etat. How you say *coup d'état?*"

"Coup d'état."

"Oh. Okay. General, he die. King find out, you know, of coup d'état. He mad—*furieux.*"

"Yes."

"But general dead. What king do?"

"What?"

"He put general—his body, you know—in prison. Ghost of general stay by body in prison, so king, he punish ghost."

The worst kind of ghost was the ghost of a suicide; he remained on the spot where he had killed himself and he was an uneasy ghost. Not many generations ago in the old Vietnam, where life was even cheaper than in the new Vietnam, a man with money, who wished to punish an enemy,

could hire a person—you would have to pay his family—to go to the
enemy's house and kill himself in front of the door, so that the ghost
would remain there and haunt the enemy and his family for ever.

Not so long before we arrived in this neck of the woods, a ghost had
walked in the hamlet. Now, of course, the villagers had much more to
fear at night than ghosts, but, on the other hand, they also had many
more of the unquiet dead to worry about.

There was a man in the hamlet whose baby daughter cried and kept
him awake so he hit her on the head with a rock and killed her. Our
interpreters thought perhaps he was crazy, but he was the father; he had
the right to take his daughter's life.

I never got to like the people of Ben Tranh as I had the people of Co
Trach. Of course they were suspicious of us because they knew that we
had left Co Trach, and they knew what had happened to the people who
had been friendly with us there. Nonetheless, as day after day went by,
and we experienced the normal give and take of our routine in the hamlet—talking together, taking pictures of the children, asking after their
health, giving them medical attention—a bond grew between us.

Sometimes I even had fun out in the hamlet—the children tried to
teach me to speak Vietnamese and they were no longer ending each
sentence with "Gimme chop-chop." The adults became friendlier. We
saw persons we had never seen before and they stayed to gossip with the
interpreters.

One of my medics said to an elderly woman, "Chao ba." ("Good
morning.") She replied and then asked the interpreter how to say "How
are you?" in English.

One day a kid pulled a new one on me. He said, "Gimme honk-honk!"

Questioning revealed that he wanted Cepacol throat lozenges—one of
the medics had constantly referred to the children's coughing as "honk-
honk." The pills tasted like candy.

The turning point in my relationship with the villagers came when I
retrieved the body of the man murdered by the VC. I became the man to
see.

They called me the Mayor of Ben Tranh and they ignored the hamlet
chiefs and the village chief. They knew if something went wrong in the
hamlet they had to come to me. We rebuilt the home for the woman who
lost her children. When the villagers went down to the river to cut reeds
to make new roofs, I informed our patrols that the villagers were there
and we should not take them under fire.

When we were determined to find a source of water out by the hamlet
so we wouldn't have to truck it in, the Bear went for a stroll through the
hamlet with a few of his staff. We weren't able to find an adequate

source, so we hired some Vietnamese to dig us a well inside Damron. Slowly, day by day, bucket by bucket, they dug a square shaft into the earth. We were gone before they were finished, but we Americans had come up with a project and hired local labor.

An itinerant barber, who went from hamlet to hamlet, came to me and asked permission to set up outside the fire support base and get American customers. He would come toward the front gate, approaching in broad daylight, showing both hands wide open, and someone would pass the word for me, and I would check him out and vouch for him, and there he would sit and cut hair. A Chinese-speaking entrepreneur came to Damron to request permission to scavenge the scrap we had abandoned throughout our AO—burned-out helicopters, trucks and tanks, or empty artillery shells. I granted it: *Insofar as it lies within my authority I grant permission to the bearer of this letter to scavenge abandoned metal along the highway.*

"How do you like being the mayor of Ben Tranh?" Lt. Logan asked me.

"I'd like it well enough," I said, "if I spoke Vietnamese."

"I thought you were learning?"

"I am. I can say *chao co, mon joy,* but by the time I know enough to do me any good, I'll be out of here. I should have started learning it at Benning."

"Then you'd be one of the adviser-pricks."

"That's true."

We could have used a language-school graduate in every platoon, but that was the MAC-V zapper—if you knew enough Vietnamese to do the job as Battalion S-5, you were not assigned to be a Battalion S-5 in a U.S. Infantry Battalion, you were assigned to MAC-V. By inadvertent policy, no member of a U.S. Infantry Battalion knew Vietnamese.

PART VIII

New Life

(15 March–19 June 1969)

From Someone Who Didn't Serve

I sometimes wonder what poor snook
Went off for me to face the gook.
Well, he'd have got deferment, too,
If he'd known the folks I knew.

I'm free and white and twenty-one,
An influential father's son—
I needn't hide, I needn't run,
Needn't learn to shoot a gun.

The unemployed and underpaid,
Here's their chance to learn a trade.
It's best I guess that Uncle Sam
Should send them all to Vietnam.

I'm free and white and twenty-one,
An influential father's son—
I needn't hide, I needn't run,
Needn't learn to shoot a gun.

Learn a trade and fight the war
And if they die, we've plenty more.
Besides the snooks are largely black—
Who gives a flip if they come back?

I'm free and white and twenty-one,
An influential father's son—
I needn't hide, I needn't run,
Needn't learn to shoot a gun.

Chapter 23

PROTECTION

The natives who worked for the Michelin Rubber Company lived in villages scattered throughout the plantation. The villages were pleasant shady places, sheltered from the sun by a canopy of palms and rubber trees. The contrast between the cool air in the shade of the canopy and the hot air outside produced a constant breeze; the huts of reed and plaster admitted the breeze and shed the rain. Each hut had a large, polished water jar outside—water had to be trucked in all during the dry season—and a table of herbs and spices. The villages had a central area set aside for meetings, church services, and plantation orders, and they all had a school and a portrait of Jolly Pére Michelin: Drink Clean Water! Bathe Regularly! Eat Good Food!

These villagers seemed singularly unwilling to give us their hearts and minds, mainly, we assumed, because if they did, the NVA would rip their gizzards out. We couldn't "protect" the villagers, scattered as they were throughout the Michelin, so MAC-V decided to relocate them in "New Life Settlements" where we would be able to "protect" them; MAC-V ordered an independent force under the command of our S-3 ("Doc" Holliday) and composed of two U.S. Infantry companies from our Battalion (Bravo and Delta), two U.S. mech companies, and a company of Arvns to relocate the people (and not allow one hair on one single civilian head to be mussed). In all we would have to move 1445 men, women, and children (110 truckloads), 51 pigs, 181 cattle, and 206 chickens and ducks.

We flew in by huey and chinook the evening of 17 March. The Arvns dug in almost as fast as we did.

"Look at them go," a G.I. said. "They must be Marines."

They weren't. They were a regular Arvn unit, but Arvns didn't need to do much to impress us—they had to be the worst troops in the world, we thought, because if they weren't, what the heck were we doing here?

We said, "Those little suckers don't do nothin' 'cept take our money and whine."

They said, "You get maybe 500 dollah, we get 50. You here maybe one year —we stay—we fight, no one year, many year, beaucoup year, all time year."

We said, "Well, Jack, it's your country."

They said, "No. We fight communism. It your fight."

"Bastards. The NVA get eleven bucks a month—when they get it—and no three-day passes."

"Those dudes won't last a month when we leave."

"What we ought to do," Speedy said, "is send an Arvn division to the Philippines and train it from the ground up—full power to promote and demote. Send them all, one at a time."

"What we ought to do," said someone else, "is annex this dump and run it the way it oughta be run. Those Arvns don't know jack-one about running a country."

"They sure do know how to make themselves comfortable though."

The night of the seventeenth we were supposed to be resupplied by the mech companies, but they had to laager at a partially destroyed bridge— the AVLB (Armored Vehicle Launch Bridge) that was supposed to get them across the creek got stuck in the ruined girders. We (Americans) didn't have any food.

I, however, dined on poulet à l'Arvn (poached). The Kit Carson and two interpreters procured a chicken, some rice (two kettles), and all kinds of vegetables. They cooked the rice in one pot and the chicken (the whole bird chopped up—bones, insides, and all, plus some little hot peppers) in the other pot. After dinner I reclined in the shade and listened to the quiet. A Vietnamese village could be a pleasant place . . . from which we were relocating these people.

Redd took a tour of the hamlet and came back with Touchberry and an Arvn interpreter.

"Guess what I just saw, sir."

"What?"

"I saw a kid walking a mouse on a string."

"Many children up here," the Arvn interpreter said, "have pets."

His English was excellent and I took the opportunity to ask some questions. Why did everyone laugh when I said *chao ong mon joy* ("Hello, sir, how are you")?

He laughed himself—I had picked up the village pronunciation and I spoke like a hick from the sticks: *Howdy dere, young feller.*

"Where did you learn your English?" I asked.

"From books."

"It's very good."

"I hope to visit your country someday."

"You can come and stay with me," Touchberry said.

In our moment of brotherhood, the interpreter smiled sadly; he knew that the sun also rises in Vietnam and it scatters dreams like the morning mist.

After the Arvn departed, Redd said, "These guys aren't so bad. It's hard to believe that, say ten years down the line, they'll all be dead."

"But will they have died in vain?" I asked.

"Of course not," Touchberry said. "They'll be under every Christmas tree—the latest coffee table book—NOW FOR THE FIRST TIME! NEVER BEFORE PUBLISHED PICTURES OF THE WAR! ALL NEW! THE DEAD IN LIVING COLOR!"

"Yeah."

"SEE THE WEAPONS OF '67. AIRMOBILE OPERATIONS. TET. ALL THE CAMPAIGNS. THE COURAGE. THE CARNAGE. CATCH IT ALL . . . FOR ONLY $4.99 A VOLUME, FIRST VOLUME SENT WITH A THIRTY-DAY, MONEY-BACK GUARANTEE."

"I'd rather read it than do it," I said.

"If I'd known what doing was going to be," Redd said, "I'd have done it to Canada."

"I can see it, man," Touchberry said, "around 1980, they'll have them on TV. 'The real heroes.' "*

"THEY CALLED THEM COWARDS," I said.

"The misunderstood youth of America," Touchberry said. "All they had with which to fight the unjust policies of a corrupt bureaucracy and callous government were their convictions."

"As it opens," I said, "we see a small child. She is speaking to her father. 'Where did you demonstrate in the last war, daddy?' "

"In the pilot episode Howard Freedom, campus radical, meets a returning black student, Joe Bisatz, just discharged from the army. Bisatz, a former Green Beret, is going to school on the G.I. Bill. Freedom convinces Bisatz that he has been the innocent dupe of the military-industrial complex."

"Yeah, and Howard Freedom's girlfriend, Melanie, convinces him to make love not . . ."

BANG!

I went for the ground. It's amazing how long it takes, even from a low

* In our wildest imaginings we never imagined that Vietnam would become a rock video.

starting position, to get completely flat, and it's amazing how much thought can be crammed into the time in transit: *That's a machine gun, ours, three grenades, ours, one scream (strangled and bubbling), theirs.*

Despite the multiple lifts of hueys and lifts of chinooks, despite the visible berms of the foxholes and the wire we had strung, despite the bunkers we had improvised and our movements in the village, despite our loud American voices, despite, in short, a presence advertised every way but Sunday—GRUNTS AT WORK—some idiot NVA had diddly-bopped to town.

Two idiots, in fact.

One was an NVA paymaster with his books: Ten cigarettes a month to Nguyen van Chi, extra ration rice to Nguyen van Truc, Nguyen van An is docked a couple pi. The other was a poet; in his pocket we found a little book, three inches by two, where he had written his poems, poetically slanted across each page. (Poor Nguyen van Yeats—in some forgotten hamlet he had had his rendezvous with destiny.) Sunny wanted that little book, but the Brigade Spook (who had come along to see what he could see) confiscated it; he didn't know Vietnamese, but he thought the poems might contain data, which, when processed, produces intelligence, as a pig, when processed, produces sausage.

The paymaster was wearing a belt buckle, a beautiful blue enamelled belt buckle with gold trim and a large red star. I wanted that buckle, but Redd asked for it and duty is duty and schnapps is schnapps, or, in other words, a good officer does not pull rank to cop the spoils, so I let him have it; Redd gave it to his medical service sergeant (who hinted that his children would love to have such a buckle).

"Well, Redd," I said, "I hope you like the field . . . because you'll be out there until you find me another belt buckle."

But I did get one souvenir—a blood-stained card:

ADMONITION TO U.S. AND SATELLITE p.O.W. s AFTER BE-ING CAPTURED

1. Don't Worry! The S.V.N.N.F.L. and the L.A.F. give lenient and humane treatment to P.O.W.s. You will not be killed, nor beaten!

2. Follow me, leave this place at once to avoid danger.

3. On the way to the P.O.W. camp, you must severely obey our orders.

4. In case of American air raid and artillery shelling, you must not run away, but follow me to cover.

5. You are not allowed to talk. Interpreters of the P.O.W. camp will talk and answer you.

S.V.N.L.A.F.

Chapter 24

THE RAIN IS NOT THE SAME

"Okay, boys," Redd said, "let's have a quiet night."

I curled up on the hard-packed dirt floor of the hootch we had chosen for headquarters, set my helmet beside me, and placed my glasses in the helmet. I woke up in the bunker, my helmet on my head and my rifle in my hands. Mortar rounds were exploding outside. I had jumped to my feet, run over sleeping bodies to the other room and into a bunker which my waking mind had noticed only to wonder how I would fit myself through the doorway, if I ever had to. Now, when I was wide awake and able to think, other men, who had not been so quick, crowded in, making the bunker a tempting target for a VC infiltrator and the mortar attack seemed to be slackening.

"Where are you going, man?"

"Out."

"Let's all get out of here," Doc Holliday said.

I returned to the other room. All was darkness and gloom, but I thought I detected a quiver in the wood frame of the bed. I looked underneath and there, his rifle pointed at the wall, was the Brigade Spook . . . babbling, "They're coming! They're coming!"

They could have been crouched just outside the wall, pulling pins from their grenades. I strained to see into the dark. Impossible to see anything. A flare burst. Light! I looked . . . but everything was blurred. My eyes! What had happened to my eyes? I touched them. My glasses were gone. Where . . . ?

Redd had a flashlight.

"Shine it over here," I said.

A thin high, panic-stricken voice cried out, "Medic! I'm hit. Medic!"

"Hang on, sir. I have to treat this man."

Where are my glasses?
I groped around the floor.
"I'm dying," the wounded man cried.
"It's just a scratch," Redd said.
Under the bed the Spook was still pointing his rifle at the wall.
"They're coming!"
"I'm dying!"
"Shut up!"
Where are my glasses?
A firefight broke out on the perimeter. Bullets struck the wall above us.
"They're coming!"
"I'm dying!"
"Shut up!"
"Call a dust-off!"
"Shine a light over here," I said.
Redd shifted the light and there were my glasses. I could see again . . . and see—thank God—nothing, though I heard a lot: M-16s, AKs, grenades, an RPD, artillery, popping flares and . . .
"They're coming!"
"I'm dying!"
"Shut up!"
"Private," I said, "if you want to be on the dust-off and not back on the line where you belong, don't say another word."
He shut up.
"Captain, get out from under that bed. The NVA are not inside the perimeter."
He crawled out.
"Redd, go into the next room and tell the S-3 you're a medic and this is now the Battalion collection point."
(I say to this one, come, and he cometh, and I say to that one, go, and he goeth.)
As the darkness lifted a G.I. on the perimeter was hit by a ricocheting bullet.
"Medic!"
Shanker (an eighteen-year-old medic with acne) crawled up and went to work. While he was working, he heard an object hit the ground nearby.
"Grenade!"
Shanker threw himself across the wounded man, the grenade exploded, a fragment smashed his kneecap. G.I.'s and NVA tossed grenades back and forth, fragments whined all around, Shanker was ex-

posed, he thought he was going to die, but, before he could decide what to do, the fight was over. A cock crowed, day was coming, and time had run out for the NVA. They ghosted away. Shanker wrapped his knee and hopped toward the dust-off. A big grin kept breaking out on his face—the wound was simple, no loss of limb, but a broken kneecap meant a medevac to Japan; he had risked his life and saved his man, despite the other medics, who had said he cared too much about himself to ever be much good.

I walked around the village. The NVA hadn't shown their usual determination—we had rather damped their enthusiasm in the last month or so—but the village looked like a battlefield: Palm trees were torn to shreds, a few hootches were blown apart, and others had burned to the ground. An old woman had died, not directly from enemy action, but we guessed that the excitement had caused her heart to fail and she was indisputably dead. Had we failed in our mission? No, I thought, because a baby had been born.

"No one was supposed to get hurt," Doc said to me.

"It wasn't enemy action."

"The woman is dead."

"But a baby was born . . ."

"But the woman is dead."

"Look, sir, we had to deliver 1445 living bodies to the concentration camps and we have 1445 living bodies to deliver.

"Right. Round them up."

Arvns roasting a haunch over an open fire invited me to join them; the roast almost looked like lamb, but where would they have found a lamb? Nowhere. It was a dog and I declined.

After breakfast hueys lifted the Arvns out to round up the village cattle. The Arvns were in a good mood.

"We're cowboys," the interpreter shouted.

We loaded the villagers into trucks; some of the villagers were crying.

"Why the hell are we doing this?" a G.I. asked. "It's their country."

"Yeah," Redd said, "so none of us got blown away, we could have, just to move a bunch of civilians to a concentration camp."

"It can't be that bad," the G.I. said.

"It will be."

"This whole country isn't worth a single one of my friends," the G.I. said.

What is worth a dead American?

Not Vietnam.

And we'd just surpassed the toll of World War I (though the baseball commissioner, if he were keeping this record book, would double-asterisk the figure:

COMBAT* DEATHS** IN VIETNAM
  *excluding disease-related deaths
  **(in a longer season),

so I asked,

"What keeps you going, then?"

Officers were supposed to put across a simple message, *we've got to stop them somewhere,* but no one believed it, neither those who heard it, nor those who said it, unless they were very, very stupid; so what did keep the G.I.'s going?

"I don't know. I ain't a lifer. I ain't gung-ho. I just can't let the others down."

An NVA soldier couldn't have put it better. As for the Arvns, well, you can't buy loyalty.

We watched the people being driven away from their village and then we clambered on-board the armored personnel carriers that were assigned to escort us down the road. APCs on the move look like prehistoric monsters; riding them is like riding a living beast. They sway from side to side. They juke and jolt and shamble along. They jerk when they turn and they slide in the mud and seem to stumble. The rainy season was just beginning, and I clung to the slippery metal hulk and imagined what a body would look like after an APC had trampled it.

We reached a fork in the road. We had to go left . . . to another village . . . in the rain . . . to the boonies . . . where the NVA ran wild. I knew it, as I knew that our base camp was to the right: Food and shelter, beer and bed, a bunker line, a roof above my head. I could almost hear the singing in the O Club. (In training when it rained the teaching staff provided shelter and sometimes cancelled the exercise.) We lurched to the right and my foolish hopes soared. We turned left and I thought, this is reality.

The sun had gone down by the time we reached the village and we had to laager in the dark. We didn't have enough men to form a tight perimeter. We didn't have wire. The S-3 said, "We'll just have to do the best we can."

He moved inside an APC. I looked around and decided, whatever else, I was going to put a solid roof above my head. In one hootch was a table with a stone top. I shifted that, added rocks and a sandbag or two to the sides, and thought I might survive casual steel.

I curled up, my gas mask for my pillow, my hand upon my rifle, my glasses in a pocket where they wouldn't be lost, and I went to sleep.

CLANG!

Something hit the table above my head.

THUNK.

Something hit the floor.

A grenade about to explode? I swung my feet in that direction, curled into a ball, and counted . . . one . . . two . . . three . . . pop! Illumination. The tube from an artillery flare had plummeted to earth atop my table.

Otherwise the night was quiet and in the morning, after I had examined the table top and the chip (the size of my fist) gouged from the table by the tube, I helped to ship the people out (they wept, too) and then we moved toward another village, this time on foot. Just as we saw the first hootches, a VC shot at us. We lay down. The point shot back. The lead platoon maneuvered—nothing to get excited about. An older Arvn patted a young, worried Arvn on the arm.

"No sweat. Beaucoup G.I."

We entered the village, collected the people, I told them the new location was paradise on earth and they'd . . . In the distance mortars fired. I heard them and the villagers heard them, too, and they shrieked and ran for their bunkers. I looked around and saw a shallow depression, hardly a scratch in the soil, and I put my head in it and wrapped my arms around my helmet and waited for the inevitable. I had ample time to remember what a sergeant once said to me,

"You dig a hole for your head, because you can take hits in the body, but not in the head."

Not today. The mortar rounds came down far away in the Ruff-Puff compound. I was almost disappointed.

Chapter 25

WOLFHOUND LIEUTENANTS

In April and May, with the removal of the people in the outlying hamlets of the Michelin to the "New Life Settlements," our Battalion operation entered a new phase. Now, if the NVA could avoid us, they did, or, if they could not avoid us, they tried to slip away from us . . . but, if they couldn't escape, they could still fight like devils from Hell.

Brigade, in recognition of the new situation (and also because the rainy season, now imminent, curtailed airmobile operations), modified our mission. We were to "secure" the civilian population and to train the Ruff-Puffs to take our place someday.

Life on the line was not pleasant. "Low belly crawlers" a rear echelon sergeant (an E-7) called the Infantry. This sergeant was in the habit of paying thanks to the Lord of Battles that he was not as other men, that is, that he was not Infantry. On 1 April he received a set of orders assigning him to a line company as platoon sergeant "in the primary MOS of 11B40" (Infantry). His lamentations were heard throughout the Battalion area.

"A mistake . . . it must be a mistake," he whimpered, and later, when he was found in the back of a storeroom, semi-comatose, a bottle clutched in his hand, still he was muttering, "A mistake . . . it must be a mistake."

It was not a "mistake." His clerks had cut the orders as an April fool's joke.

Platoon sergeants' lives were apt to be nasty, brutish, and short in any case, but one platoon sergeant, in Lt. Roe's platoon ("C" Company), had a more specific complaint:

"The lieutenant's trying to kill me."

"Well," I said.

"I'm not joking," he said.

He was more afraid of Lt. Roe than he was of the NVA.

"That Lt. Roe," Captain Ervin said. "I tell him what I want done and then I never have to think about it again."

When Lt. Roe took over his platoon, he told his men that he expected them to carry the "basic load" plus one LAW (Light Antitank Weapon) apiece. And that was that, until, one day out in the field, he noticed that his men were not carrying their LAWs.

Why not, platoon sergeant?

You didn't tell me I was the one supposed to make 'em.

Lt. Roe took his platoon for an extra stroll that day . . . a circuit outside the wire around Dau Tieng. The platoon sergeant and the squad leaders each carried a 90mm recoilless rifle and every man carried one 90mm round. No one ever again forgot the LAW.

Lt. Roe decided to train his platoon sergeant in combat duties, in which the lieutenant thought the sergeant was deficient. He sent him out on ambush one night. Inside Damron we could hear the explosion of the claymores and the burst of small arms.

"That lucky S-O-B," Lt. Roe said.

He got the sergeant on the radio.

"Five, this is six. Over."

"Six [came a hoarse whisper], this is five. Over."

"What do you have? Over."

"Six, I don't know. Over."

"What do you mean, you don't know? Sweep the killzone. Over."

"There may be some wounded NVA out there. Over."

"Sweep the killzone. Over."

Long pause.

"Five, this is six. Have you swept the killzone? Over."

"Six, there's activity out there. Over."

Lt. Roe was exasperated.

"Five, sweep the killzone . . . or do you want me to come out there? Out."

The bystanders and the eavesdroppers enjoyed themselves immensely.

Touchberry said, "Who do you think is hoping more he doesn't come out, the sergeant or the NVA?"

Touchberry was one of the most popular men in the Battalion. He was always cheerful and upbeat.

"The army's not so bad," he would say. "It's the first time I had all I wanted to eat and a bed to myself. It'll pay my way to college, maybe even med school, which I could never even have dreamed about before the army."

Touchberry was the second person in Vietnam I cried for.

On 9 April in the Iron Triangle, Chico (a platoon leader in Bravo Company) led his platoon (the point platoon) into a bunker complex. The bunker complex was so well camouflaged that no one in the platoon recognized what they had stumbled into and Chico and Touchberry sat down to lunch on one of the bunkers, which they thought was just a rise in the ground. The NVA were there, but they did not want a fight with us. When, however, the platoon did not move on and more troops seemed to be coming, the enemy were afraid they would be trapped, and they opened fire.

Chico was hit in the feet and knocked down. Touchberry ran to him, to give him aid; he was shot in the head and killed. From where he lay wounded Chico directed the firefight for six hours, until a dust-off could get in and take him to the Division base hospital.

Touchberry had not been armed. The NVA knew he was a medic; they saw that he was running to help a wounded man, and they shot him. Violence is answered with violence. Bravo Company volunteered to go back into the Iron Triangle to avenge him.

We hired Cambodian mercenaries and paid them strictly on results—captured weapons or proof of body count. (The proof they preferred to give was a severed penis.) The mercenaries were part of CRIP (Combined Reconnaissance and Intelligence Platoon). The CRIP lieutenant, named Smith and nicknamed Speedy, was on his second tour.

In December we had been ordered to trade our recon platoon to the 2/12 Infantry in exchange for their CRIP. The idea, and not a bad one, was to leave in place the platoon that knew the area, but we had to exchange Wolfhounds for whatever the 2/12 were and we lost the recon platoon leader, Lt. Davis.

Colonel Reese (with the new CRIP lieutenant present) had said, "We are losing an outstanding lieutenant . . . but I am sure we are gaining a good one."

Lt. Davis and his men showed up at the 2/12 with the Wolfhound crest on their shoulders. A 2/12 administrative sergeant told them they would have to remove the crests.

"Try it," Lt. Davis said.

When the Battalion commander visited them, the men snapped to attention, saluted, and said, "First Wolfhounds, sir!"

As the original members of the platoon rotated home, Lt. Davis indoctrinated their replacements in the Wolfhound way. He suffered for this lèse majeste. The 2/12th kept him on line until he had fourteen days left. Then he was allowed to return to us to await D-ROS.

"Once," Lt. Davis told me, "they ordered us to put out a checkpoint with my platoon. *We suspect an NVA regiment might be moving along the road disguised as farmers. Watch for them.* Sure enough, here they come. I reported . . .

" '. . . a large number of men dressed as farmers.'

" 'Roger. Check them out.' "

The "farmers" had wagonloads of hay. Were men and weapons concealed in the hay? Lt. Davis was canny—he took no chances he didn't have to take. He ordered his platoon to spread out and bring all their weapons to bear, while he, by himself, walked forward to meet the "farmers." The "farmers" were young men—and, therefore, suspect—but no weapons were visible. As the first cart came abreast of him, he flicked his zippo and set the hay on fire. The oxen broke into a trot. *Cheoi oi* the "farmer" exclaimed and ran after it. The others picked up the pace and trotted past Lt. Davis, as he flicked his lighter again.

"I never was sure they weren't VC."

Our own CRIP, by now pure Wolfhound, lived in a separate compound just south of Dau Tieng. Speedy (originally a platoon leader in "B" Company) had made the compound as comfortable as possible— their own PX, a club, showers, brick bunkers/living quarters. The Arvns, G.I.'s, and Cambodian mercenaries lived there in apparent amity.

The Cambodians were tough cookies; their work was their pleasure, life meant nothing to them . . . , and a visiting general tried to rip them off. The general was doing the tourist bit, he rather fancied the pistol a mercenary had, and he suggested that the mercenary give it to him.

When the Cambodian refused, a staff sycophant (major) tried to grab it. (Speedy said, "He didn't ask me or I would have told him.") The Cambodian was too quick. He drew the pistol, chambered a round, and aimed it at the major. The other Cambodians raised their rifles and released the safeties. Click! Click! Click! The major jumped back.

"Can't you control your people, lieutenant?"

"Hell no, sir," Speedy said. "They'd kill you as soon as look at you. And," he added, ever the diplomat, "they don't like thieves."

Speedy told me afterwards, "I've never punished a mercenary and, if I ever have to, I'll kill him. You leave him alive, you're just asking to get a bullet in the back."

I recalled his words often during *l'affair Pup*. Pup was a grunt who loved to walk point.

"I just stick a shotgun round in my M-79 and off I goes," he said. "Don't even got to sniff the others' sweat."

And when he found a bunker, inside he went, before you could say tripwire. He loved tunnels. He loved having his own supply-issue .45. He loved jacking a round into the chamber of the .45 and sliding down, head first, out of sight.

"You never know. Could be anything down there, could be buried treasure, could be a gook nurse. And I got a nose for 'em."

No one expected him to last the tour. His lieutenant was concerned. He'd had almost two months without a kilo.

"Jeez, Pup, don't spoil my record."

"I gotta see it happen, sir."

When Pup grew short, the lieutenant tried to save his life by assigning him to the rear of the platoon.

"And, Pup, stay there."

But when the firing started here Pup came . . . on the bounce.

"Where they at? Where they at?"

Everyone liked Pup ("that crazy bastard"), so when we discovered the source of his courage—bags and bags of sweet green chaff hidden in his gear—we quietly confiscated the greenery and put the question to him, "Just tell us where you got it, Pup, and we'll let you go."

The RVN bunker.

Of course.

I undertook a formal investigation, which elicited the following note:

From Ngo - Van - Suong
    Kit Carson Scout
    "D" Company
April 21st 1969
To:
    Captain Bradford
    (S-5 commanding)
Sir,

On April 20th 1969, (while) I went to make clear the road with "D" Company when I came back the hootch I'm lost my barrack-bag that contained two suits of clothes, two towels, two undershirts, and two undertrousers, specially my 3500 piasters were lost, too.

I didn't know who took all my things but on April 12th I saw The who stole one GI's radio in the bunker, moreover, when he came to the hootch by honda, he usually took cigarettes in medic hootch (S-5).

Those were all bad-attitudes therefore I wanted to report to you and depended on your idea may check and help me!

Please don't let everybody know.

Thank you sir.

The Kit Carson scout, named The, was fencing stolen radios, tapedecks, and cameras to Vietnamese in exchange for dope, which he then sold to Americans. (Their excuse to steal was always you have so much, we have so little.)

"Okay," the Bear said. "What I want to know is this, are the village officials implicated?"

"They didn't start it, but they took a cut."

"Okay. Let's nail the scout."

We raided the hootch, impounded the evidence, and sent the scout packing. The officials moved to town.

A couple of weeks later, when I was riding in the back of a truck along a more civilized road than the one running to our FSB, I saw The again. He was on a motor scooter and he had a pistol. He rode along beside us for a while. He looked at my hands, which were both on my rifle (the rifle's safety was off); our eyes met and then he turned away and rode out of sight.

A few weeks later I was asked to visit an outpost on the road. A sergeant had noticed a new face among the Coke girls and he had laid his hand upon the point of anatomical truth—his squad believed that he was copping a feel. He discovered a little deception. The girl-who-wasn't pushed him, jumped on a motor scooter, and tried to escape; the sergeant had a straight-away shot down the middle of the road, plenty of light, no distractions, and no need to hurry. The bullets knocked the impostor end over end.

"I think I've seen him," the sergeant said to me, "but I don't know where."

The dead face looked like a cheap plastic reproduction (as all dead faces do), but I recognized it.

"Remember the Kit Carson scout who fenced the radios?"

"Oh yeah," the sergeant said. He nudged the body with his foot. "Well, boy, you sure went the long way round to die, didn't you?"

Chapter 26

DI CU CHI

In late April the Bear took me aside and said, "I think it's about time we had a talk. How's civic action doing?"

Fine, I was able to say. I showed him a form which I had developed (out of a civic action publication) when we first arrived in our AO—and before I had begun to ponder the moral intricacies of working, albeit indirectly, for Saigon. The form had twenty-seven questions and each question had to be answered "yes" before we could call a hamlet "secure."

At my first survey (in December) I could answer yes to only three questions: 24—yes, *there are serviceable roads to the hamlet;* 25—yes, *local sources of water are adequate;* and 27—yes, *military incidents have not adversely affected relations with hamlet.* Now, at the end of April, I could answer the questions as follows (and this is the form that I showed to the Bear):

DEPARTMENT OF THE ARMY
1ST BATTALION 27TH INFANTRY
(THE WOLFHOUNDS)
25TH INFANTRY DIVISION
APO 96268
SUBJECT: Hamlet Control Checklist
AVDCSU.F

Tri Tam	Thanh An	Ben Tranh
district	village	hamlet

YES N☒☒ 1. Local government exists.
YES N☒☒ 2. Military control of the VC has been broken.
YES N☒☒ 3. External VC units have been reduced up to 50%.

YES ~~NO~~   4. Only sniping and mining occurs on routes to the hamlet.
YES ~~NO~~   5. Most Party apparatus is identified.
YES ~~NO~~   6. Effectiveness of Party apparatus is curtailed.
YES ~~NO~~   7. No overt VC incidents have occurred within the last month.
~~YES~~ NO   8. Local communications system is operative.
~~YES~~ NO   9. Friendly forces meet security requirements.
YES ~~NO~~ 10. Hamlet chief is receiving useful information from informants.
~~YES~~ NO 11. GVN managerial groups are usually present at night.
~~YES~~ NO 12. Census grievance program has been completed.
~~YES~~ NO 13. Civic associations are being developed.
YES ~~NO~~ 14. Full time medical support is rendered by external teams.
~~YES~~ NO 15. Formal full time education is available.
YES ~~NO~~ 16. Some welfare needs are being met.
~~YES~~ NO 17. Economic programs are underway.
~~YES~~ NO 18. People have consented to self-help projects.
~~YES~~ NO 19. Some participation in self-help projects has been achieved.
~~YES~~ NO 20. District forces are 75-100% authorized strength.
~~YES~~ NO 21. VC are unable to operate during hours of darkness.
YES ~~NO~~ 22. VC do not collect taxes.
~~YES~~ NO 23. Local defense groups exist.
YES ~~NO~~ 24. There are serviceable roads to the hamlet.
YES ~~NO~~ 25. Local sources of water are adequate.
~~YES~~ NO 26. The hamlet officials are not corrupt.
YES ~~NO~~ 27. Military incidents have not adversely affected relations with hamlet.

He glanced down the list.

"Most of the *no*'s, it seems to me, the Arvns have to change to *yes*'s."

"Yes sir, I think so."

"For instance, number 26—*the hamlet officials are not corrupt.* Do they think we're in Oz? All RVN officials are corrupt."

"Yes sir."

"Hell, Saigon can't answer that question *yes*."

"No sir."

"Okay, then. I think we've done just about everything we can in Ben Tranh. Good job."

"Thank you, sir."

"Now I want you to spend your time in the Michelin."

(Thanks!—"Hey, Redd! Hey, Nooyan! Guess what? We're going to the Michelin.")

I gulped and said what had to be said.

"Yes sir?"

"I want you to move to the CRIP compound and go out with them."

Speedy liked to load his men up in their trucks, add a unit of the 170th Ruff-Puffs, and hit the roads. One of his trucks mounted a minigun, another mounted a .50 caliber machine gun. He drove all over the Michelin. He set up check points, he searched hamlets, he put out ambushes—he could have fed, clothed, and armed CRIP with what they had captured.

I—and my two medics, Redd and Nooyan—were supposed to travel along with him and convince the Vietnamese civilians: *All is the best in the best of all possible worlds (and will be even better tomorrow). Be good, be patient, support Saigon.*

So we moved from Damron and travelled the Michelin with Speedy. The Michelin was as quiet as the Michelin could be. We found a mine occasionally and once a sniper fired a round in the air over our heads, but otherwise we went where we wanted when we wanted without opposition and even with some support.

In one hamlet I recognized a child wearing an RVN T-shirt (the part that isn't red is yellow) and I recognized his mother. They had lived in Co Trach.

"Hey, I know that woman. Why'd you move, mama-san?"

She shook her fist.

Grenades! Artillery! Rockets! Small-arms fire! NVA! The noise and the flares and the danger. No sleep.

"Didn't Charlie object to you moving?"

Let him! What did she care for Charlie? Booby traps for children! Thieves in the night, stealing rice!

"You tell 'em, mama-san," I said and thought (with wonder), *we're getting somewhere,* and then a Ruff-Puff traipsed by with a chicken dangling from his hand.

"VC," he said, "all VC."

We should have put him against the wall right there and shot him, but MAC-V told us: *They know best how to treat their own people.*

The bastards.

Speedy's two Arvn interrogators had evolved their own particular method of gathering intelligence. They took the best looking girl in the village off by herself into a hootch, one of them grabbed her nipples, and the other interrogated her—*a good-looking girl like that, shoot, man, her sweety must be an NVA officer.*

Wherever we showed up, there, inevitably, we found a Chinese-speaking entrepreneur (who had requested permission to scavenge our scrap and so had our permission to go where he pleased). Once he asked me, with a contemptuous jerk of his head toward the Ruff-Puffs, "What for you bring these people?"

"Well . . ."

"Too loud. Always shout. Americans are quiet, gentle."

I couldn't disagree, even if, as I suspected, he was NVA psyops.

The NVA had a fertile field for their propaganda in the New Life Settlements. The New Life Settlements were horrible: They had no gardens, no bushes, no trees, nothing green on which to rest the eyes, only dust, heat, and concertina wire. The living quarters had been slapped together from plywood and sheet metal and then divided into cramped, stifling cells. ("Much better than these people are used to," the MAC-V adviser told me.)

The only medical care they received came from me and my medics. At first, when I visited the compounds, our new battalion surgeon accompanied me.

"How old do you think this little girl is?" he asked me.

"I don't know—six or seven?"

"She's twelve," he said. "Put your hand on her abdomen."

She grinned as though we were playing a game.

"Press gently."

I could feel a lump the size of a softball.

"If the growth isn't removed, she'll never get any bigger."

"Can it be removed?"

"Sure, if the mother takes her to the hospital."

We explained it to her. She shook her head. You go to the Arvn hospital, you don't come back.

These people had good reason to suspect the government. The district government had promised, if the people moved to the settlements, they would be given twenty sheets of tin, $VN7000, and eighteen grams of rice a day. The government delivered seven sheets of tin, $VN2000, and, once, a handful of cooked rice. In addition, the Ruff-Puffs hassled them, stole from them, and threw CS in the compounds.

We Americans secured the compound to the south of Dau Tieng; we guarded it by day and ambushed it by night. The Ruff-Puffs secured the compound to the north of Dau Tieng. The NVA entered the north settlement at night, gave the people food, showed them movies, and treated them with dignity. *You think,* the NVA said to the villagers, *if the Americans win, you will have Americans here, but you are wrong. You will have Arvns.* They also suggested that, perhaps, if all went well in the near future, the people would be able to return to their hamlets. The people cheered.

When I went to the settlement to win some hearts and minds by pass-

ing out Arvn balloons and patting babies on the head, an old man dod-
dered up to me, touched my Battalion crest, and muttered in a questioning tone, "Woof'oun?"

I nodded.

He yelled and all the villagers disappeared into their bunkers.

"I think they're pacified," Redd said.

The villagers were afraid. Under questioning I picked up the rumor
that the NVA were planning something big. We increased our patrols
and on 10 May a company of Wolfhounds made contact. The NVA tried
to break away, but the Wolfhounds forced them to stand and fight.

The Bear pulled another company right from the field and lifted it
directly to the contact. Brigade ordered other units into the area under
the immediate direction of the Bear. By nightfall we had formed a perimeter around the NVA. All night the artillery fired H&I inside the perimeter, while the NVA tried to escape. In the morning a company of Wolfhounds was ordered to sweep the area. (Before they were through, they
counted ninety-seven enemy bodies.)

"For God's sake, take a prisoner," the Bear commanded.

We wanted more information about this supposed NVA major offensive, but the attitude of the company was, "They wants to play, they gots
to pay."

The Bear pleaded and threatened, so did Brigade, and, finally, the
company succeeded in nabbing a prisoner. The prisoner confirmed the
rumor. His unit had been moving to their assembly point, the offensive
was to be launched the next night, the night of the twelfth. Speedy decided to try to ambush elements of the NVA as they approached their
assault line. He said to me, "Go to the lookout tower if the NVA break
through," and then he led two-thirds of CRIP out on ambush.

That night the NVA attacked 159 fire support bases and base camps,
among them Cu Chi, Dau Tieng, and the Ruff-Puff Compound, but they
attacked neither CRIP nor Damron. The attacks failed, but the NVA had
a different version to spread in the hamlets and the compounds.

I visited a hamlet that had been visited by the NVA. A boy almost of
military age—he thought I wouldn't understand him—said to me, "Di Cu
Chi."

Go to Cu Chi.

The NVA had spread lurid tales about their attack on Cu Chi—every
American had been killed; the airfield was a mass of flaming wreckage;
the base had been abandoned.

Di Cu Chi.

I laughed.

"Sunny," I said, "set him straight."

I meant, speak to him, tell him the truth, and, if he doesn't believe it, maybe we can arrange to take him there, a witness against us, to see for himself that the NVA had lied.

Sunny had different ideas; he slapped the boy across the face.

"That'll teach him," the adviser said.

You bet.

But the problem of Dau Tieng was to be our problem no longer. During the eight-month operation (24 October 1968–9 June 1969) we had almost daily contact with the NVA, our fire support base was assaulted three times, we had established four independent forts, and we had accepted the surrender of dozens of VC and NVA. The VC who came over helped us destroy the infrastructure of the Dau Tieng area. In February and March we had lost twenty-seven men and we had killed more than four hundred NVA soldiers. In all we killed close to a thousand NVA—the destruction in detail of an NVA unit larger than our own.

The road (on which our convoy had had to fight every day, going and coming, for five weeks) had become so quiet that the Bear rode up and down in his jeep, our interpreters and scouts went back and forth to town on motor scooters, and entertainers—and staff tourists—drove out to visit us. We had "secured" and "pacified" Ben Tranh and large parts of the Michelin. The NVA had had enough of the Wolfhounds. Division decided that we had accomplished our mission and now should move on.

On Wednesday, 9 June 1969, a battalion of the First Division took over Damron. They were a bit nervous about the whole affair, and they should have been, because they were overrun that night. ("Those sneaky little bastards," a G.I. said, referring to the NVA, "they sure used their Wolfhound training.") Within a year the District Chief was ambushed and killed on the road we had opened and secured.

The Wolfhounds had a stand-down in Dau Tieng. Refitting and recreating. At the Officers' Club No-Nose played the guitar. The surgeon sang, "I don't want to be a soldier," Yodeler sang, "There's a long, long trail a-winding," and the chaplain sang, "What a friend we have in Jesus." Then the FO sang "Hi, Gene!" the song we had written about Mac, or, as we called him, Lt. Eugene Maclecher, and his hootchmaid, and the chaplain left. I was ordered to sing a solo.

"I'll probably bring the roof down," I said and launched into "Let Me Call You Sweetheart."

BAM!

A rocket hit outside the club and a large chunk of the ceiling fell. We fled to the bunker.

"The Flying S-5 sings no more," our surgeon said.

PART IX

What Was It All About?

The Gas Station (A True Story)

I stopped at a station to fill the car.
A woman came out and pumped the gas.
"I've had to pump the gas," she said,
"And shovel snow, and mow the grass,"

"Because my son's in Vietnam.
I don't know where. He sent a map,
But all those funny names—Duk Wok.
Du Lap, Suk Nao—I can't read Jap."

Chapter 27

BACK IN THE WORLD

In forty-eight hours I went from a combat zone in Vietnam to my home in Appleton, Wisconsin. I dumped the contents of two dufflebags on the floor of the living room—suits and cameras from Hong Kong, silk and bronze cups from Thailand, medals and an odor from Vietnam. My father wanted to touch me to reassure himself that I was there, and he wanted to hear about it: What had happened, what was it like, were we winning, what did it all mean?

I said, "It doesn't mean anything. The whole thing isn't worth one dead American."

I had been awake for forty-eight hours. When I finally got to sleep, I dreamed I was in Vietnam. I saw three lieutenants, my friends, who had died there.

"We want to live," they said to me.

I dreamt about them every night for a week. When I stopped dreaming about them, I felt as though I had betrayed and abandoned them.

The first night home I woke at three. I thought someone had called to me with a shout, "Captain!"

I looked out the window. There were no NVA in my backyard. I went down the back stairs into the kitchen and made coffee. My father got up and joined me, not to talk, but just to be with me at three in the morning for coffee.

For days I stayed up late, slept fitfully, dreamed of the dead, woke early.

Then one night I heard a footstep on the back stair. NVA! My heart pounded. But I was in my own bed in my own home. Perhaps I had dozed off, perhaps it was a dream . . . or had I heard a burglar? I was shaking, I moved as slowly as though I were in a dream . . . until I put my hand on the revolver in my desk. Immediately I was calm. I walked to the head of the stairs and flipped on the light. The stairs were empty.

"You fool," I said to myself. "You must have been dreaming."

But, I replied, *it had sounded so real.*

"Relax. Go back to bed."

All right, but I'm not letting go of this revolver.

I lay in bed and stared into the darkness until I heard the footstep again. I flipped on the light again and again I saw nothing.

Am I going crazy?

I waited. I *had* heard a footstep . . . or I was crazy . . . or the dead do rise (but we can't see them with the lights on).

Was I going to be one of those veterans who goes out for a cup of joe, has a flashback, and wastes a cafe full of people?

A mouse came out from under the stair, reached up with its front paws, grasped the next step, pulled itself up, slipped, fell . . . thud. The footstep.

When I told this story to a friend, she asked me, "What would you have done if someone had been there?"

"I would have shot him."

"Just like that?"

"What else?"

What else?

Anyway, I wasn't crazy and I had found a cure for my insomnia. I kept a revolver where I could touch it when I roused in the middle of the night. The revolver even appeared in my dreams and resolved all my nightmares . . . except the one in which I was on a plane going back *there*.

I tried to pick up my life again, to visit friends of previous days, but Vietnam always intruded. When I went to see one friend, my best friend, and I bounded in the door to say hello, an AK went off behind me. I went to the floor and so did a table of drinks, chips, and dip. The TV was featuring film clips of the PLO at target practice. Welcome home!

I took up hunting again. I had always enjoyed duck hunting, the cold before dawn, the aroma of the slough, the sun coming up, and the elusive mallard. Now I found that the mallard was not so elusive anymore. I heard, or saw, the ducks before they heard me, or saw me, and I sneaked up on them. *Boo!* They leaped into the air and I shot them. Hunting was no longer a sport.

In the middle of October, not long after the opening of duck season, my vision suddenly blurred and I had a headache like a hammer blow. My doctor sent me to a neurologist.

"Have you been under stress recently?" the neurologist asked me.

I had already told him that I had been in Vietnam.

"Well," I replied, "it's no fun having people trying to kill you."

He thought he had found a classic case of paranoiac delusion, but after a further discussion of this and that and Vietnam, he deduced that I was suffering from migraines brought on by a release from tension. I had a migraine every two weeks through November, one a month through February, and one last attack before the summer.

Migraines. Nightmares. Insomnia. I had to sleep with a revolver and I had to sleep in a small secure room. Little noises woke me—a mouse eating birdseed two rooms away—and when I heard loud noises, I ducked, or ran for a bunker. I drank too much. I was angry and I felt as though I was always on the verge of violence. In an argument with a stranger in a bar . . .

He said, "I'm from South Dakota. It really gets cold there."

I said, "Well, I'm from Wisconsin and it gets colder here."

"Oh yeah?"

"Yeah."

. . . and I was checking where the pool cues were.

In the midst of trying to come to terms with myself, I decided to go back to the University of Chicago to complete my doctorate in classical languages and literature. The chairman of the Classics Department was a veteran of World War II. Before the war he had lived in Paris, driven a cab, and boxed with Hemingway; now he shaved his head and kept a .45 in his desk drawer. A graduate student, who had just taken the doctoral examination, said to him, "Mr. Bruere, I don't know what I'll do, if I fail. I'll probably kill myself."

Mr. Bruere reached into his desk drawer, pulled out the pistol, and said, "This department is ready for anything."

I felt comfortable at Chicago.

Up in the Nonesuch Coffee Shop the three of us who were veterans would drink our coffee and talk; sometimes other students joined us.

"Yup," I said, "it's obvious. I would put one machine gun in this window, another across the street."

"Good final protective fire in case Hyde Park ever goes to war."

I said, "My question is, are politicans or reporters bigger slime?"

"You were an officer, weren't you? We enlisted men had a third category."

"My great aunt died," one of the veterans said.

"Yes?"

"My mother's mother's sister. My mother wanted me to feel something. I asked her, 'What am I supposed to feel?' "

"What does it mean?"

"It don't mean a monk."

"Epictetus says, *if the room is smoky, leave it,*" said a student who was not a veteran.

"Meaning what?"

"Meaning that the only choice under our own control is the choice to end our life, if life is unbearable—everything else is out of our control. We can never be happy until we accept that."

"I learned to accept that it happened and to get on with things, but I never learned not to care."

"That's his point. If you could, you would acquire philosophical serenity."

"Or I'd have to be drunk all the time."

In the summer I stayed at a cottage on a lake in the woods of northern Wisconsin, alone except for an English Setter. The woods, the water, and the isolation helped me to heal, but I still needed the revolver and I still had nightmares. (I asked a veteran of World War II when I could expect the nightmares to end and he said that he would let me know.) I dreamt that a dark shape was at the foot of the bed. I woke. The shape was still there. I reached for the revolver . . . before I realized that the dog was asleep and unconcerned. I looked again and the shape dissolved.

My first summer home I had to go to an Army Reserve Camp at Camp McCoy. I got my first haircut since leaving the army . . . from a World War II veteran of the 32nd Division, Bob Arndt—"I was a corporal going in and a corporal coming out; the best rank: Too high to do KP, too low to have responsibility."

When the Chinese invaded Vietnam, Bob and I both dreamed we were back in the Army. During the Indian-Pakistan war I found myself driving toward the front in a jeep, seeing the dead, analyzing their uniforms and their equipment, and suddenly I knew—whoa!—that I was getting way too close to the fighting. The dream was so vivid that I thought of writing an article on it—Your Reporter at the Front.

Periodically I would wake up on the floor of my room in Chicago. I didn't know why, until one night as I was about to doze off I heard mortar fire—in-coming!

Now is that really likely, I said to myself, as I went to the floor. *In the heart of Chicago?* The sound of the elevator doors closing was vaguely reminiscent of a mortar . . . if you were half asleep.

My experiences did give me some advantages. I could understand ancient authors at a level denied to students who had not seen the elephant.

"Like, for instance?" a student asked.

"Take Archilochus. Here's this guy, from the island of Paros, twenty-seven hundred years ago, makes his living as a soldier, the illegitimate son of an aristocrat, and a poet."

"More like a songwriter or a rock star."

"We just have fragments of his work."

"And none of the music."

"Right, but one of the fragments . . ."

"You mean, 'So what if I threw my shield away. I will live to fight another day?' "

"No. I mean 'We chased seven and killed them . . . the thousand of us.' "

"What's to understand?"

"There was a joke at Benning—'We were surrounded, our whole company, we fought all night, pinned down, I thought we'd had it, until at dawn in desperation we attacked hand-to-hand and we killed them all, all three of them.' It's the punchline of a joke."

Since I knew that a twenty-five year old G.I. could go to Hawaii for an R&R with his third wife, hop a plane to California (illegally), *visit* his second (divorced) wife in California, move on to Georgia and *visit* his first (divorced) wife, return to Hawaii for some more time with his third wife, return to Vietnam only to discover that he had picked up a *bug* from his first (or second) wife, a *bug* which he had probably passed on to his third wife, whom he now intended to divorce because she had not written to inform him that she had *the bug* and so probably thought she had gotten it somewhere else, I could hardly be surprised at the activities of Messalina or Poppaea. Since I knew that a G.I. could shoot a prisoner "because it's fun," I could hardly be surprised that Nero executed a wealthy man to raise cash for a game of dice.

"You ever read any Ardrey?"

"*Territorial Imperative?*"

"Do you believe that society trains us to be violent?"

"I believe that aggression is a part of human nature, as Aristotle says."

One of our medics, a conscientious objector, had been brought up in a religion which taught that violence is learned behavior. He was excused from all weapons training on grounds of religion. He had never handled a firearm in his life. In Vietnam one night while his company was set up in a peaceful hamlet in a pacified area the NVA struck. He was in a hootch working on a wounded man when an NVA soldier with an RPG on his shoulder appeared in the door. The medic grabbed the wounded man's M-16 and shot the NVA soldier dead. In a split second without conscious thought he killed another human being. Other medics tried to console him. *If you hadn't done it, he would have killed you and your guy. You had the duty to save your guy. You had the right to save yourself. And, anyway, it's not like they're human.* The medic had passed his whole life believing that humans were corrupted by society, that those raised in his religion did not turn to violence, that he was truly Christian, but now, if he could kill another human being, he must not be truly Christian, and if he was not truly Christian, then he would go to Hell.

"Vietnam was a blue-collar war."

"It sure wasn't the *Iliad*."

Glaucus, why are we two honored above all others in the feasts in Lycia with all we want to eat and drink, and why do all look upon us almost as gods, and why do we possess rich orchards and fertile fields along the river? Must we not stand first among the Lycians whenever we go into battle, so that some one of the heavily-armored Lycians might say, "Not unjust is it that our kings hold Lycia, eat the fat hams and drink honey-sweet wine; they prove their right when they fight among the first ranks of the Lycians."

"At least in the city-state the rich also ran the risks and went to war and paid for the running of the state."

"How long do you think the war would have lasted if Senators' sons had had to go?"

"How long do you think the war would have lasted if Senators had had to go?"

At the University of Chicago I learned to read Latin and Greek texts and to analyze what I had read. I learned to think clearly and to express my thoughts clearly. I learned the substance of ancient history and in the process of studying that history I learned, as much as I ever could, to understand the human condition. I felt ready to pass on what I had learned to others.

Chapter 28

THE WILL OF THE PEOPLE

I received my Ph.D. in 1973 and immediately threw myself into the job market with blithe confidence. And why not? When I received my M.A. in 1966, I had been offered a position at a university in my home town (an offer I had to decline because I expected to be called to active duty at any moment) and now with a Ph.D. in hand I expected a flood of offers. I was lucky to get a one-year, half-time position.

My first job was to teach a survey of the history of the ancient Near East and Greece. Ancient Greece presents a microcosm of human behavior—political life on a small scale where the results of government decisions are immediately apparent—and its history is far enough removed from us that we can view it with detachment. The Greeks are interesting on their own terms, but as an undergraduate field of study they are more important for what they teach students about themselves; I asked my students questions of war and peace: Who should make the decision? who should pay for the war? who should risk his life? what are the effects of wars? why do nations and peoples go to war? are there war heroes or only victims? can war ever be justified? is war more than the expression of a human propensity to violence?

In the context of Greek history I was putting questions to students that I had put to myself ever since Vietnam. I was not ready to teach a course on Vietnam itself—I hardly could, since years would go by before I could say the word *Vietnam*—but, as a service to the ROTC detachment, I created a military history course, *The Ancient Art of War*. The commandant asked for more.

"My guys aren't going to learn much from ancient warfare—all line battles. Swords. Shields. Command was simple."

"War is simple," I said, "if you know where the enemy is and you aren't exhausted, and you aren't scared . . . but you don't know, you are exhausted, and you are scared. The Greeks were, too."

He pressed me to attend a seminar at West Point where I would learn how the Army teaches military history and then I could transmit the authorized version and technical vocabulary to my students. I grew tired of saying *no,* so I finally agreed to go, and I can't say that I'm sorry I went. I liked the officers I met and I enjoyed the seminar, but I came away with serious reservations. Vietnam has influenced the thrust of military history all out of proportion to its historical importance; the preoccupation with the reasons for our failure in Vietnam and the search for excuses have focused military history at West Point on such questions as "the media and the military," "politics and the military," and, in particular, "the will of the people."

General Westmoreland referred to the issue of *the will of the people* in a lecture he gave us. He hates reporters like poison and so do I (when I think about Vietnam). For him the defining moment of what the media did to the war effort came in a conversation with Lyndon Johnson. Walter Cronkite had just returned from Vietnam and had spoken out against the war. Johnson said to Westmoreland, "I have just lost middle America." General Westmoreland's reaction was, how shameful it is that the American people would give more credence to a newsman than to their President.

The media did do a poor job in Vietnam. Reporters took the easy story: They listened to what the generals said and then they wrote the opposite. They stayed in Saigon and appointed themselves our spokesmen. They knew little about Vietnam and they didn't try to learn more. Senior correspondents came on a two-week tour of Southeast Asia and returned to the United States as certified "experts." They made public potentially harmful information. (A popular magazine printed an aerial photo of our fire support base.) Yet the reporters' war is the war American students know: The war was misconceived, badly fought, and the American soldier was the villain; all Americans committed atrocities, we shouldn't have been there, the VC/NVA (no distinction drawn between them) were patriots (much like colonialists in our War of Independence), and the only American heroes were those opposed to the war—in a word, reporters.

On the other hand, historians both in and out of the military cannot even agree on the questions to ask about Vietnam, let alone any answers. Did we lose a war or just not gain our principle objective? (The military is only now admitting that maybe we did lose.) Could we have won? Did military leadership fail at the top? Was there a lack of strategic planning? Should there have been a formal declaration of war? Should we have invaded North Vietnam? Did we misunderstand the nature of the war, that is, believe it to be a revolutionary war when in fact it was a conventional war, or, conversely, believe it to be a conventional war when in fact it was a revolutionary war? How did we (the military, that is) lose the national will? Was the media responsible? How and to what extent could the media be controlled in time of war? Can a democracy such as ours fight long wars?

Out of this fog of history have come three principles of policy (applied most recently in Desert Storm):

1) Have a clear—and obtainable—objective.
2) Don't fight a war you won't go all the way on.
3) Keep the war short or you will lose the American people.

First, as a professional historian, I reiterate that Vietnam has been emphasized far too much. When Vietnam is placed in the context of the Cold War, many of the Vietnam issues disappear. The "failure of national will," for instance, must be balanced against the willingness of Americans to support war-level military forces (and the concomitant expenditures) for forty years during the Cold War.

When we began our involvement in Vietnam, our motto was, "You gotta stop 'em somewhere," or, as a friend in the CIA wrote me, "You are fighting this little war against them now so that we will not have to fight the big war here later." Historians of the future may well analyze Vietnam as follows: As soon as the United States determined that it was fighting a local war unrelated directly to the larger struggle, it made the decision to disengage. Disengagement may be inglorious but wasting one's resources—not to mention killing one's fellow citizens—in a sideshow is foolish, debilitating, and self-defeating.

Historians of the Vietnam generation, both military and civilian, have invested the phrase, *the will of the people*, with altogether too much significance. Unless the historian considers that a war must end in the death of every adult citizen of the losing side and when it does not, it does not for the sole reason that the will of the losers has been broken, the historian can find few wars that have been lost through a failure of the will of the people. Germany and Japan fought long after reason would have dictated that they should concede defeat. Examples of a failure of will often turn out to be a failure of leadership. In the French collapse in the battle of the Ardennes the senior French officers—the regimental and division commanders—abandoned their troops. In ancient Greece, where the citizens were the army, a failure of will really would have ended a war, but the pattern of Greek history is rather that the losers fought until they could fight no more and often took the victors down with them.

Secondly, as a veteran of the fighting in Tri Tam in '68–69 as well as a historian, I have another perspective on *the will of the people*. Our initial mission was to interdict the enemy supply routes in Tri Tam. The mission was expanded until in effect we were charged with the pacification of the whole of Tri Tam. We outfought the enemy, destroyed the VC infrastructure, drove the NVA underground, gave hope to the villagers (or, more bluntly, convinced them that we were going to win), opened the roads, brought back local government (for good and ill), and supported and trained the provincial forces; and yet we were directed in our operations by Brigade command as though our mission were to fight the NVA main forces and nothing else. Brigade ordered us to move from Mahone to "Damron" in a tactical adjustment of our position for the purposes of better artillery support. When we moved, we handed Co Trach back to the NVA; they convinced the villagers that they had defeated us and forced us to retreat. They reeducated the local Vietnamese who had begun to trust us and support us.

Similarly, when we were ordered out of the district of Tri Tam, Tri Tam was lost. We believed at the time—and I have seen nothing to change my opinion—that we were being ordered out of Tri Tam because of higher command's fixation on body count. As we began to dominate the NVA in Tri Tam and they became reluctant to fight us, our body count dropped. As our body count dropped, pressure mounted from Brigade (and on Brigade) to increase it. In other words, because we had been successful we were judged to be failing and the more successful we were in pacifying our area of operation (hence the lower the body count), the more we were judged to be failing in our primary mission.

Tri Tam was the war in miniature, and we understood Hanoi's strategy in Tri Tam no better than we did for the whole of Vietnam. We outfought them. We convinced them that the cost of fighting us was too high. We forced them to suspend operations so long as we remained in the district of Tri Tam, but we couldn't—or wouldn't—stay for the long term, the Arvns were incapable of replacing us, and the NVA were allowed to bounce back. We knew what had to be done. I told the Brigade S-5, "We need to have a unit permanently stationed in the village."

"We can't do that."

"Then we can't pacify the village. You can't pacify terrorized people."

"You're the S-5 there—it's your job to find a way to do it with the resources you have available."

Part of the pacification checklist was to extend Saigon control (i.e., "local government") into the villages. We did it, but we knew that what we gained in points in the rear set us back in the field—the blatant corruption of the village officials drove the villagers back to the VC. Saigon could rule only at gunpoint and the guns were ours.

With apologies to General Westmoreland, if he had known what we out in the field knew—and he should have known it—he would have recognized that he was using American forces to impose upon the South Vietnamese the sort of government that he would have fought to the death to prevent from being imposed on us. Admittedly a career officer does not climb up the promotion ladder to that first star by telling his superiors that he cannot, or will not, carry out their orders—or that their orders are both impossible and immoral—and a general does not become a commanding general by contradicting his commander-in-chief. (The names given to the traits thus produced are *loyalty, obedience,* and *duty.*) In almost all circumstances an officer's duty is to obey his superiors; in Vietnam, by attempting to impose a corrupt and despotic government on the South Vietnamese in the name of freedom and anticommunism, General Westmoreland was promulgating a lie, he was living a lie, and he was allowing the President to live a lie.

Those of us in the field knew that Vietnamization was a sham and a lie. We were ordered to put our lives on the line for it. We did, but we also knew our leaders were lying to us and that we could no longer trust them (though we did obey them). Our true loyalty was to each other and our true mission was survival. Soldiers no longer said, "Ya gotta stop 'em somewhere," they said, "I can't let the others down." (This is not to say that we thought Hanoi would be any better than Saigon, but only that it would be equally bad in a different way.)

We had our solutions ranging from the outrageous—annex Vietnam, kick the Vietnamese out, and resettle the place with Americans—to the impractical—pull out the 25th Arvn Division, send it to the Philippines, train it from boot camp to staff college, cashier inefficient officers and non-coms, promote without reference to family connections and influence, and send them back to our area of operation where we would train them, test them, promote and demote, and turn them into a unit capable of fighting the NVA; then we could begin the process with another Arvn division. This solution was impractical because we would have given the boot to members of the class with which our leaders identified.

Anyway, as things were—and forgetting for a moment that Vietnamization was shameful, that Saigon was corrupt, and that the Arvns couldn't do the job—in Tri Tam we didn't even have Arvns. We had Ruff-Puffs and we knew that the Ruff-Puffs could not then or ever replace us, and that when we withdrew they would run—we knew that but no one above us wanted to hear it. They wanted to hear, "They can hack it." If

we told the truth, that the Ruff-Puffs couldn't do it, then . . . "I guess
you've failed in your mission, haven't you, mister?" . . . and our careers
—those of us with careers—would suffer. Career officers, if they valued
their careers, were forced to live the lie.

Politicians may live by the ancient precept, "There is no difference
between the truth and a lie, for men utter both to gain some end," that is,
you say what you need to say in order to convince your audience to do
what you want them to do, but the lie we were ordered to live by was not
that kind of lie. It was a ruinous, self-deluding lie based on the acute
realization that if Vietnamization were really true, then we were okay,
but if it were not true, then we hadn't a clue what to do, and therefore it
must be true and we will punish anyone who says different.

The lies came home to roost. Despite politicians jumping on the band-
wagon of superpatriotism—*I back my President, I back the boys in uniform, vote for me*—despite the military chiefs clicking their heels while
repeating the litany, *yes sir, yes sir, no excuse sir,* despite the ego of two
presidents who could not admit they had made a mistake; despite these
persons, when veterans returned to the United States and denounced the
lies, both big and little, then the "leaders" of this country lost *the will of
the people,* and, as military historians put it, "when you lose the will of the
people, you lose the war."

Many military men (and some veterans) still believe that Hanoi used a
clever campaign abetted by American reporters to undermine and erode
American will. Given the circumstances, given the world view under
which we became involved in Vietnam—the monolithic Red Menace, a
Soviet satellite in Southeast Asia—given that we had lost direction mili-
tarily; that one President had concealed the costs (in money) of the war
and another had promised a chimerical "solution'; that Vietnamization
was a fantasy; that Saigon was more corrupt than Hanoi and hardly less
tyrannical; that our leaders, political and military, either lied directly or
by implication or else supported the lie with their silence, we need not
wonder that the American people repudiated that leadership and its war.

There is a misconception about leadership, a misconception not limited to the military, that loyalty is a one-way street running from subordi-
nate to superior. On the contrary, loyalty has to be earned. The commander who gives impossible, contradictory, or immoral orders forfeits
the respect, trust, loyalty, and sometimes the obedience of his subordi-
nates. Long after the war was over, several senior military leaders began
beating their breasts: Oh, how they had agonized over their decision to
support their President; oh, how they wished they had either resigned or
spoken frankly about the war, but their oath, their loyalty to the commander-in-chief, etc., etc., etc.

Their point seems to be that agonizing over doing what lay in their own immediate interest and for their own immediate profit makes it okay; for me, the lesson is that they had a fundamental misconception of where their loyalty in the service of the United States should lie. As long as military officers confuse their loyalty to their country with their obedience to their commander-in-chief, they will also confuse the *failure of the will of the people* with the failure of the people to agree with them. This perception—that when the people disagree with their leaders the leaders are right, the people are wrong, and the national will is lost—is false. The sovereignty of the nation rests in the people—*we the people of these United States.* We delegate power to our representatives, but they only *represent* us; when they put their own self-interests before the interests of the whole people, we have the right to repudiate them.

The real *will-of-the-people* lesson from Vietnam is this: The American people will not long support a misconceived policy costing American lives, no matter how much our "leaders" favor the policy and no matter how committed those leaders are to it.

EPILOGUE

My eight-year-old daughter Elizabeth asked me, "Daddy, why did you do it?"

My students ask me the same question (between *were you hit* and *did you grease anybody*).

Vietnam was my generation's adventure. I wanted to be part of that adventure and I believed that it was my duty as an American, both to serve my country and particularly not to stand by while someone else risked his life in my place. I do not regret my decision to go, but I learned in Vietnam not to confuse America with the politicians elected to administer America, even when they claim they are speaking for America, and I learned that I have a duty to myself and to my country to exercise my own judgment based upon my own conscience.

About the Author

Alfred S. Bradford is an Associate Professor of History at the University of Missouri-Columbia. He earned his Ph.D. in classical languages and literatures from the University of Chicago. He served with 1/27th Infantry (Wolfhounds) of the 25th Infantry Division in Vietnam, September 1968 to August 1969. He was awarded the Bronze Star, Air Medal, and Purple Heart. He is the author of *Philip II of Macedon: A Life from the Ancient Sources* (Praeger, 1992).

He is the John Saxon Professor of Ancient History, Department of History University of Oklahoma, Norman, Oklahoma 73019-0315.